PEACE UNDER HEAVEN

PEACE UNDER HEAVEN

Ch'ae Man-Sik

Translated by
Chun Kyung-Ja

Introduction by
Carter J. Eckert

An East Gate Book

M.E. Sharpe

Armonk, New York   London, England

An East Gate Book

Library of Congress Cataloging-in-Publication Data

Cha'e, Man-sik, 1902–1950
[T'aep'yŏng ch'ŏnha. English]
Peace under heaven / Chae Man-sik : translated by Chun Kyung-Ja
p.   cm.
ISBN 1-56324-112-9 — ISBN 1-56324-172-2 (pbk.)
I. Title.
PL991.13.M3T313   1992
895.7'33—dc20
92-31807
CIP

Cover illustration by Lee In Su

Printed in the United States of America
The paper used in this publication meets the minimum
requirements of American National Standard for
Information Sciences—Permanence of Paper for
Printed Library Materials, ANSI Z 39.48-1984.

∞

BM (c)   10   9   8   7   6   5   4   3   2
BM (p)   10   9   8   7   6   5   4   3

Contents

Acknowledgments

The translator would like to thank Professor Kim Sung for his invaluable help without which a number of textual passages in the idioms of the 1930s would have failed to receive faithful interpretations. Thanks also are due to Professor Kevin O'Rourke for his willingness to comb painstakingly through the entire manuscript twice, offering good suggestions for worthier renderings of many lines of dialogue. Another who deserves mention here is my husband, Dr. James West, whose training as a lawyer did not entirely incapacitate him from aiding me in trying to do justice in English to Ch'ae Man-Sik's inimitable style. Thanks as well to the friends who provided encouragement at various stages of the project in 1989 and 1990, to Douglas Merwin of M.E. Sharpe, Inc., to Professor Bruce Cumings of the University of Chicago and to Professor Carter Eckert of Harvard University. Last, but not least, I am grateful to the family of the author, Ch'ae Man-Sik, for their consent to undertake this project back in 1987.

C. K. J.

Introduction

In *Peace Under Heaven* Ch'ae Mansik (1902–1950) has fashioned a brilliant black comedy of many meanings. It is a work that is historically specific to Korea's colonial past and also universal in its human understanding and appeal. It is a work whose concrete and precise descriptions of people, places, and events are suffused with ironies that are simultaneously funny and appalling. It is, not least of all, a tragicomic story of the sudden fall from grace of one of fiction's most unforgettable, larger-than-life characters. It is all these things and more.

With so many approaches to this great novel, now splendidly rendered into English by Chun Kyung-ja, it would be presumptuous for me, especially as an historian, to offer anything suggesting an authoritative literary interpretation. Everyone will have his or her own favorite reading, and one of the communal delights to Korean studies in the classrooms and colloquia of the future will be to discuss and debate various aspects of Ch'ae's work. Nevertheless, *Peace Under Heaven* has given me such unmitigated pleasure that I am unable to resist a brazenly pre-post-modernist attempt at explanation, however personal and impressionistic. Caveat lector. Those readers who wish to keep their minds pure and unconstructed are advised to ignore the following and move on immediately to the actual text.

For the intrepid few who are still with me, let me begin with a couple of observations about *Peace Under Heaven* as a window into Korea's experience under Japanese colonial rule (1910–1945). Although Ch'ae was not writing for the benefit of future historians, and the novel neither can nor should be reduced simply to an historical document, it is nevertheless a fascinating source of information to anyone interested in Korea's early twentieth-century past, a period so close in time to our own and yet in so many ways still so hidden and elusive. Ch'ae's novel provides, among other things, a rare glimpse into the urban landscape of the late 1930s, when Seoul was Keijō, Shinsegae (Sinsegye) Department Store was Mitsukoshi, and the wealthy classes, including many absentee landlords from the Chŏlla provinces, were ensconced in Kyedong. It is a world of rickshaws and streetcars, young schoolgirls in blouses and bows, harried busgirls, *kisaeng** and *kisaeng* guilds, prostitutes on Kwanggyo Bridge and in the Tonggwan red-light district, radios and gramophones, Tanp'ung cigarettes, the Festival of Great Singers at Pumin Hall in front of the Government-General building, the movie *Morocco* (starring Marlene Dietrich and Gary Cooper), and extended mahjong parties for the idle rich. The novel's authenticity stems not only from its author's North Chŏlla background and reportorial skills honed during years of writing for various Korean newspapers and magazines, but also from its contemporaneity. The story takes place on September 10–11, 1937. The novel was first published as a

---

*See glossary.

serial in the monthly magazine *Chogwang* beginning in January 1938. Without necessarily intending it, what Ch'ae has done is to capture and preserve for us a brief moment of colonial time.

It is also worth noting that Ch'ae's colonial world, described from the inside, is psychologically far more complex and intriguing than the ex post facto colonial history we have been taught and are still teaching today. Accustomed to narratives of poor and heroic Koreans struggling against rich and evil Japanese, we find ourselves suddenly disoriented, even overwhelmed, by the sheer range of Korean personalities and private feelings, by no means always attractive, that Ch'ae lays out before us. Human voices wake us, as Eliot said, and we drown. Ch'ae's work should be a welcome challenge to all of us who write Korean history. It is time we threw out the ideological stick figures who still populate most of the monographs and textbooks on the pre-1945 period and looked more to literature and personal testimony to help flesh out and humanize the existing statistics and documents.

To focus solely on the question of historicity, however, would be to ignore the novel's primary value as an important work of literature. Ch'ae Mansik is justly famous in Korea for his satire and irony, and *Peace Under Heaven* is one of his masterpieces. The immediate object of Ch'ae's formidable wit in the novel is the absentee Chŏlla landlord and usurer Yun Tusŏp, better known as Master Yun, who lives in the Kyedong area of Seoul with an extended family consisting largely of women. In the course of the novel Ch'ae takes us on an often hilarious day-and-a-half excursion into the mind and life of his chief protagonist and some of Yun's relatives, retainers, and victims.

To say that Master Yun is an egoist is like saying Confucius was a philosopher. Yun's egoism is colossal. His succinct guiding principle, consistently observed, is to "let everyone else go to hell." His entire life has been spent pursuing and protecting his own interests, and now, at the age of seventy-two, he is fabulously rich and, thanks to the order and stability of Japanese colonial rule, the great "peace under heaven," Yun is secure in his fortune and at liberty to enjoy his own personal "peace."

"Peace" for Yun consists, first of all, in doing more of the same: preserving and enhancing his wealth. Yun is an extraordinary miser. Not a single *chŏn* is given up without a battle, whether with his family, his favorite *kisaeng,* a busgirl, or even with an unlucky rickshaw-man who mistakes him for a generous customer. With an income of over one hundred thousand *wŏn* per year (including ten thousand bags of rice from his own land-holdings), he still berates his family for not diluting the dinner rice with barley and keeps them dressed in shabby clothes. Only when it serves one or another of his personal passions, such as promoting his grand-son's bureaucratic career (and therefore his own sta-tus), is Yun willing to part with some of his money, but even then he makes every effort to keep the amount as small and painless as possible.

But he does indeed have other preoccupations, and his wealth allows him to give them free rein. One is an obsession with social standing. The son of a low-life country gambler, Yun is determined to acquire *yangban* aristocratic status for himself and his family. When the story opens, he is already well on the way toward his goal. He dresses in the finest *yangban* attire, complete with horsehair hat and a silver dog-head cane, lives in a large traditional home with a gate as large as the capital city's own South Gate, has more or less successfully married off most of his children and grandchildren to impoverished *yangban* families in need of his money, and has even purchased the gentlemanly title of "Master" for himself from a needy local Confucian school. In Yun's mind all that now remains to crown his ambitions is for his two grandsons (both with *yangban* mothers) to follow time-honored aristocratic tradition and receive appointments to high positions in the government bureaucracy. To insure these goals, a county magistracy for Chongsu and a police chief's position for Chonghak, he continues to spend considerable sums of money on his grandsons' education and advancement. Chongsu, however, we come to discover, is something of a disappointment. He is, in fact, an amiable but totally unambitious fellow, given to wine, women, and as much of his grandfather's money as he can get hold of, but Yun is so eager to secure the county magistracy for the family that he continues to support him. In the meantime, Yun stakes his hopes on his younger grandson Chonghak, the future police chief, who is studying law in Tokyo at his grandfather's expense.

Yun is also much concerned with his own health. Although in rare moments of reflection, he suspects he may have only about another ten years to live, it is clear that he really hopes to live forever. To that end he exercises regularly and consumes large quantities of Chinese medicine, ginseng, wild boar and deer blood, and reindeer antlers. But even feeding off expensive plants and animals is not enough. He also takes an old folk belief seriously and arranges to have delivered to him every morning a fresh cup of steaming child's urine, obtained by contract from a poor family in the neighborhood. Whether because Yun's stratagems for longevity are working or simply because the "wonderful world" he is so loath to leave continues to sustain and invigorate him, Yun is indeed the very picture of robust good health. He is huge, at least six feet tall, with an "immense behind" that is the bane of rickshawmen and their vehicles, and despite his age, he is strikingly handsome and has the complexion of a young boy.

He also possesses, in Ch'ae's words, a "virility of barbarous dimensions." His youngest son, the illegitimate and retarded T'aesik, is the same age as Yun's great-grandson Kyŏngson and the product of a liaison with a country winehouse girl when Yun was nearly sixty. Yun, in fact, requires a steady diet of young women, a habit acquired from years of ravishing peasant girls on his country estates. Now in old age, his preference has turned to even younger girls, those barely into puberty, and his obsequious retainers are constantly on the lookout for little girls in the city whose parents' abject financial circumstances work to Yun's advantage. When we enter Yun's life in September 1937, his latest sexual fixation is a wily child *kisaeng* named Ch'unsim, whose age, fifteen, is exactly the same as T'aesik and Kyŏngson's. The interactions between Yun and his child lover, a couple as unlikely as a "hippo" and a "fox," or as an "enormous steamship" and a "tiny toot-toot tug," are among the most unsightly, and also the most humorous, episodes in the novel. At times they seem to be a grotesque parody of the playful lovemaking scenes in *Ch'unhyang*, a parallel that is strengthened by Ch'unsim and the classical heroine sharing not only the same age and profession, but also, in part, the same name.

Ch'ae's work can be read and enjoyed simply as a

mordant comment on human egoism and depravity without reference to Korean history, but it is likely that he had other things in mind as well. It is not difficult, for example, to see the novel as an implicit critique of Japanese colonial rule. The very term "peace under heaven," whose roots go back to the *Book of Rites*, has a definite political connotation in the sense of peace maintained through good governance, and in satirizing Yun and his "peace," Ch'ae is indirectly mocking the Japanese occupation that allows men like Yun to prosper. There are also a number of ironic references in the novel to Japan's "splendid" new war in China following the Marco Polo Bridge Incident of July 1937, to Japan's protection of Korea from "socialist devils," and even specifically to "this wonderful world," this "peace under heaven" that Japan has wrought in Korea and for which Koreans should be forever grateful. One might also argue that Ch'ae would have taken a more explicit anti-Japanese, perhaps even pro-socialist, stance in his novel had he not been subject to the constraints of the colonial censors and police.

While all this may be true, one can hardly fail to note that the novel's real focus is not on Japanese, but on Koreans, more specifically on Master Yun. *Peace Under Heaven* is by no means either a fascile condemnation of Japanese imperialism or a sentimental exploration of Korean victimization. While it may have been Japan who first brought "peace under heaven" to Korea, there were also Koreans like Yun, Ch'ae seems to suggest, who were willing to embrace and take advantage of it. It is not that Yun is necessarily anti-nationalist or pro-Japanese. Nothing in the novel allows us to pin such a tag on him. He has no political ideology. His only concern is self-interest. He may despise socialists as robbers who would take away his money, but he is also disgusted with the colonial government for imposing rent controls on landlords to alleviate tenant discontent.

At another level Ch'ae also seems to be implying a causal link between Korea's unhappy fate and the corruption and decadence of a moribund aristocratic society. Just as the reality of Yun's "peace under heaven" makes a mockery of the term's classical meaning, so too do Yun and his household constitute a travesty of the ideal Confucian *yangban* family. In that sense they represent the final stage of aristocratic decline, reminiscent of that moment in Proust when the indefatigable parvenu Mme Verdurin becomes the Princesse de Guermantes, and the world is turned upside down.

In Ch'ae's fictional world as well "everything is turning upside down." Yun himself, of course, is a complete *yangban* sham, and as "Master" of the local Confucian school, he reduces classical philosophy to the question of whether Confucius or Mencius would have won an imagined arm-wrestling match. Language and social relationships are also perverted. Chongsu regularly addresses his father's friend Pyŏngho in the most vulgar terms, but Pyŏngho, equally contemptuous of traditional proprieties, not only takes no offense but is eager to play the lucrative role of Chongsu's pimp and lackey. Within the family too, harmony and filial piety are replaced by a "certain etiquette of battle" as each relative wages his or her own war against Yun or other members of the household. Yun's own twisted sense of morality even allows him to curse his son and grandson for their lack of filial piety in failing to provide him with a suitable concubine. The physically and mentally deficient T'aesik, the last of Yun's sons and his father's favorite, epitomizes both the family's and the culture's ultimate degeneration. In a scene that is a wonderful burlesque of a Confucian father and son, T'aesik spouts obscenities while Yun looks on with delight, marveling at the "verbal facility of his little son."

Women also figure prominently in *Peace*, and here too Ch'ae seems to be striking out against what he considers the debased reality of Korea's late traditional Confucian culture. Indeed, at times, despite occasional asides that would today be considered blatantly sexist, he even appears to question the fundamental patriarchal values of Neo-Confucianism itself. At a certain level, the frustrations and machinations of Ch'ae's women, especially Ch'unsim, are amusing, but the dark irony of their situations is never far below the humorous surface.

All the women in the novel are more or less subject to a stifling and abusive environment that values them only as objects of masculine purposes and pleasure. Ironically, the concubines and *kisaeng* are in a sense freer and more powerful than their upper class counterparts, sequestered in the women's quarters of their homes and abandoned by their husbands. Thus when Okhwa, the concubine of Chongsu's father, pays a visit to the Yun household, she looks with barely disguised contempt upon Yun's two granddaughters-in-law. Kyŏngson's mother (Chongsu's wife), however, while thinking to herself, "What filth!" is nevertheless simmering with envy as she looks at Okhwa's expensive clothes and jewelry and considers the concubine's relative freedom. One gets an even clearer sense of the value of such freedom in Ch'ae's funny and poignant description of Yun's daughter, the Seoul Mistress. Only twenty-eight and already a widow of eleven years (after xviii / Peace Under Heaven

only one year of marriage), she is by custom basically confined to the house and forbidden to remarry. After more than a decade of such life, the mere mention of the name of her father's business manager, Taebok, the only man outside family members she ever sees, is enough to spark in her an involuntary shiver of sexual excitement. The irony of ironies here, however, is that concubine and *kisaeng* are free only by becoming, as Master Yun himself puts it, a man's "favorite utensil."

If Ch'ae disparages the traditional culture, he has, if anything, even more disdain for modernity. It is modernity, in fact, that he cites as responsible for turning everything upside down. But what does he mean by modernity? In a general sense he seems to equate modernity with Westernization, as introduced to Korea by Japan. But in a deeper sense modernity seems to signify for him a displacement of humanistic, communal values by a rational calculus based entirely on self-interest and monetary profit. Thus the world becomes a marketplace of buyers and sellers, and human beings themselves are turned into living commodities to be bought and sold.

Ch'ae mocks this new world throughout the novel. He suggests, for example, that Ch'unsim's simultaneous relationship with Master Yun and his great-grandson makes perfect economic sense "from a modern standpoint," given the current "crisis of supply and demand" stemming from a shortage of suitable women. Brothels are no longer simple dens of pleasure. They are sophisticated "universal trading companies" with a wide selection of products: schoolgirls, widows, concubines, housewives, busgirls, actresses, salesgirls, and so forth — whatever the customer desires.

For all his dislike of Western music, food, and

clothes, Master Yun is of course very much a modern man by Ch'ae's definition, and his success in the world can be attributed in part to his affinity for the new spirit of selfishness and greed. Yun's logic throughout the novel is, in fact, impeccable, even brilliant, once one accepts the basic premise of unequivocal self-interest on which it is based. Much of the humor in the story stems precisely from Yun's rationalization of his outrageous acts. When the poor rickshawman to whom Yun refuses to pay the usual fare points out that the Master was an unusually large and heavy load to bear, Yun, who is virtually incapable of thinking beyond himself, angrily retorts that it was "excruciating for a man of my size to endure your tiny rickshaw." Later, Yun's Chŏlla tenants are subjected to the same kind of relentless logic when they dare to ask for rent reductions after a major flood has destroyed their fall rice crop.

What, finally, we may ask, is Ch'ae's solution to the problems he has posed? Some readers may find in his work an indirect argument for socialism. Others may see only nihilism. I would suggest that Ch'ae's answer to the temper of his times is much simpler: to laugh. To be sure, his laugh is often sardonic. But he is always more of an observer than a partisan, and by laughing, and forcing us to laugh with him, he manages to avoid the utter despair of the nihilist, even in the absence of any tangible hope.

The true power of Ch'ae's work lies in a rich and comic sense of humanity that transcends any ideological category, and there is no better proof of this talent than Master Yun himself. Yun is unquestionably a kind of monster. One is reminded of Falstaff, "so surfeitswelled, so old, and so profane." But Yun, again like Falstaff, is also a *human* monster, and however hard we try, we cannot despise him without qualification. In part this is because he is so ludicrous, and our laughter serves to dissipate some of our contempt. But another reason is that Ch'ae never demonizes his characters. On the contrary, like a great *p'ansori* artist, he draws us into their minds and emotions, and we are compelled to see and understand each in his or her own terms.

Thus even Yun is never merely a caricature. His parents, though hardly paragons of virtue and charity, were nevertheless murdered by robbers, and this trauma provides much of the psychological context for his obsession with "peace under heaven." An expert at taking advantage of others' weaknesses, he is himself vulnerable to manipulation by his family, by his lackeys, and even by ambitious little Ch'unsim. Although his motto is to "let everyone else go to hell," and he observes it religiously, he also seems to exhibit a genuine affection for his retarded son T'aesik. Finally, in his quest for "peace," however perverse, Yun is so absolutely sincere and dedicated that in the end, when it all falls apart, one cannot help experiencing an unexpected instant of sympathy. Granted, it is a moment that quickly passes. But in that flash of human recognition by the reader, even Master Yun, depraved creature that he is, assumes a certain tragic dimension. Perhaps Ch'ae, like Shakespeare with Falstaff, never consciously intended it so, but such is the genius of great writers and the stuff of great literature.

Carter J. Eckert
Harvard University

PEACE UNDER HEAVEN

Master Yun's Route Home

The harvest festival was past and the autumn sun was going down.

Old Master Yun, renowned in Kyedong for his wealth, was just returning from an excursion. The rickshaw had halted in front of his house and he was about to get down. For the rickshawman—whether the result of bad dreams the night before or of a quarrel with his wife that morning—it had been a most unlucky day. Pulling the rickshaw along the flat had been bad, but pulling it up several hundred feet of sharp incline after turning into the narrow alley had been enough, exaggeration aside, to make his tongue fall out. The old man weighed two hundred and forty pounds and then some!

Ch'unsim, the little bitch, had discovered his weight two days before on a stroll along Ch'in Hill when Master Yun stepped onto one of those newfangled scales in front of a Western druggist's across from the back gate of the Seoul Post Office.

The rickshawman may have been born into the class of nobodies, but professional training is a wonderful thing: somehow he managed to scrape together enough energy to keep dragging that rickshaw along. At long last he dropped his harness in front of the old man's gate, a structure only slightly smaller than the great arch of South Gate, and successfully removed the rug that had been covering the old man's knees.

Master Yun exercised the utmost caution as he gingerly lifted his immense behind from its place of confinement and began to climb down. The unsteady rickshaw seemed about to flip over at any second.

"Hey, you!"

Incapable of safely dismounting on his own, Master Yun was forced to turn to the rickshawman for help.

"Don't just stand there! Give me a hand, can't you?" he growled. Actually, the rickshawman was not just standing there. He was catching his breath and mopping the sweat from his forehead. On being reprimanded, however, he felt somewhat guilty and hurriedly extended his arm to help the old man down.

Once on the ground, Master Yun recovered his full dimensions, revealing himself to be a man of great bulk indeed. In fact, an embrace, were it attempted, would more likely than not require a good armful and a half. Moreover, he was at least six feet tall. To give you a better picture, it can be noted that the rickshaw looked like a toy beside him and the gate began to tremble and quake long before he passed beneath it.

His face, too, was well preserved. Thanks to a steady intake of reindeer antler, wild boar blood, and deer blood over a period of some thirty years, plus the habitual use of ginseng and Chinese herbs, his sanguine complexion resembled a young boy's. Just the right amount of snow-white whiskers adorned his handsome face, and his general health was obvious. The corners of his eyes, sloping gently upward, looked like those of a phoenix. He had a well-proportioned nose with a solid bridge, drooping earlobes, and an ample mouth—all signs of wealth and longevity in a man.

His age? Seventy-two this year. One should not be too hasty in drawing conclusions, though. Apart from a touch of a cardiac asthma, his general health was good enough to embarrass a thirty-year-old— in whatever respect you might choose to compare them.

His appearance was another thing by no means to be sneered at.

The clothes he wore were tailored in the finest ramie. Lightly perched on his head was a splendid horsehair hat, an authentic *T'ongyŏng kat,** complete with the best trimmings money could buy. On his feet he wore comfortable cotton stockings and perfectly fitted black leather shoes. In his right hand was a stylish cane capped with a dog head of pure silver, and in his left a beautiful folding fan with thirty-four bamboo ribs. In the old days the figure he cut would have bespoken a status of no less dignity than that of a county magistrate, but alas, in the present lamentable situation it led foul-mouths to take him for a clown and candy peddlers as far away as Tokyo to salivate at the approach of a sucker.

Having stepped down from the rickshaw, Master Yun was about to adjust the wide-open front of his overcoat, but he stopped himself and untied his sky-blue purse, one of the old sort that hung dangling from his waist.

"What do I owe you?"

"Whatever you please, sir!"

The rickshawman bowed deeply, the rug wrapped around his waist. It was his usual manner of address, used indiscriminately to all customers who even slightly resembled gentry. But his humility in addressing this grand-looking old man was sincere. In other

---

*See glossary.

words, he was hoping for a generous fare.

"Uh-um! Is that so? In that case, you may be on your way!"

After staring straight into the rickshawman's face for a moment, Master Yun turned away and closed his purse. Bewildered, the rickshawman scratched his head, wondering whether the fare was to be on credit.

"Shall I return tomorrow then, sir?" he asked.

"Tomorrow? Why come back tomorrow?"

Master Yun's mood had already been spoiled by an earlier unpleasantness, and by now he was showing unmistakable irritation at having to quibble with the rickshawman. From the latter's point of view, however, it seemed clear enough that the reason for coming back was to collect the fare. But he couldn't afford to be so impudent as to state this point-blank to the old man. In the circumstances, he found himself trapped. The old man, displaying no trace of understanding of the agony of the other, was slowly beginning to turn away, as if nothing more remained to be said.

The rickshawman, totally mystified by the old man's behavior and alarmed lest the lung-bursting labor of an entire day melt into air right before his eyes, couldn't help coming to the momentous decision that this was no time to remain an indecisive imbecile.

"Well, sir, there's this matter of the fare," he blurted out with a nervous giggle. The momentous decision, in the end, resulted in nothing more than this momentously meek reminder.

"Fare?"

"Yes sir!"

"How dare you!"

Master Yun, suddenly livid, stepped forward as if he might rain blows on the rickshawman at any moment.

"You just told me to do as I please, did you not?"

"Yes sir!"

"Right. And doing as I please means the matter is left entirely to my discretion, does it not?"

The rickshawman finally grasped the old man's intention. Now that he realized what the old man had in mind, he was simply tongue-tied. It's not everyone you can joke with, he thought. In different circumstances, he might have shrugged the matter off with a chuckle, but such behavior would have been unseemly in front of the old gentleman. So he just grinned.

"I took the matter under deliberation. Do as I please, you said, and, well, I thought it was all right not to pay, so I told you to be on your way."

The rickshawman thought for a moment that the old man must be joking, but as Master Yun finished speaking, nothing in his facial expression or in the tone of his voice revealed any such intent.

"My goodness! I thought I'd run into a true marvel of a rickshawman; I judged you very well behaved. An exceptional man, I thought, who out of sympathy for an old man had offered a free rickshaw ride. Look here, young man, how can you lie so easily? Duplicity in words bespeaks dubious parentage. Yes, truly, your mother must have been given to loose conduct."

Being but a lowly rickshawman, he may not have known he was being cursed with a maxim of the esteemed Confucius— "Duplicity in words bespeaks dubious parentage"—yet he couldn't help feeling indignant at the aspersion on his mother's morals. Even though he was unsure whether the old man seriously intended not to pay the fare, the badgering was beginning to get to him, and now, on top of everything else, the old man, like a hired pallbearer roughly bouncing the coffin about, was calling him a liar and slighting his dead parents.

The fact is, if an ordinary man had acted that way on being set down in front of a thatched house, nine times out of ten the rickshawman would have slapped his face.

"Now, now, sir, there's no reason for a gentleman like you to act this way toward a man like me. A bit of paper money and you can send me on my way."

The rickshawman, hiding his injured feelings, was unerringly respectful in all he said. The words "paper money," however, were as much of a bombshell to Master Yun as any proclamation by that worthless German bastard Hitler, or whatever his name was.

"What! Paper money? What do you mean? What in the world . . . ?"

"A single one-*wŏn* note, that's all. Heh, heh."

In the face of Master Yun's outburst of disbelief, the naive rickshawman had taken him literally and had responded accordingly.

"Good heavens, I never heard anything so ridiculous. A man who just told me to do as I please, as if he had no intention of taking the fare, now demanding a one-*wŏn* note? I'm dumbfounded. . . . All right. It'd be easier to snatch a lollipop from a child than to get a free ride from you. How much do you want, then? Speak up, right now!"

Concerned that he might lose other customers if he wasted time trying to squeeze too much out of the old man, the rickshawman felt compelled to cut his demand in half; he asked for only fifty *chŏn.* Master Yun, however, was unmoved.

_____

*See glossary, under *wŏn*, for explanation of currency.

"Look here! Are you trying to pick a quarrel with me? You're wasting your breath, you know. 'Fifty *chŏn*' rolls off your tongue as easily as a child's name, eh?"

"I'm not asking for much, sir. Didn't I bring you all the way from Pumin Hall, sir?"

"That's precisely what I mean. I could spit as far as you carried me, and here you are demanding fifty *chŏn!*"

"I'm not asking too much, sir! Besides, a man of your stature might be expected to add a little something for a drink of *makkŏlli.**"

Master Yun ignored these remarks and turned to one side, once again unfastening the purse he had knotted tightly only moments before. Eventually he removed two ten-*chŏn* coins, scratching the edge of each with his fingernail. Men have been known to err from time to time, so Master Yun made it a rule to double-check all coins— the absence or presence of a sawtooth edge reliably alerted him in case he had mistaken a fifty- for a ten-*chŏn* coin.

"Here you are. I was going to give you fifteen *chŏn*— not a *chŏn* more— but since you're being so difficult about it, I'll give you twenty. With the extra five you can have that drink you wanted, strong or weak as you like. That's not for me to know!"

"It's not enough, sir!"

"Not enough? Twenty is not enough, you say? Look, young man, in a country village, twenty *chŏn* will buy you forty *p'yŏng** of land, forty *p'yŏng* of land, you hear!"

The rickshawman felt a strong temptation to snap at the old man: to tell him to go down to the country himself, buy forty *p'yŏng* of land with that twenty *chŏn*, and have the next three or four generations of his fam-

*See glossary.

ily eke out a living there. But he managed—just barely
—to stifle the urge.

"You've got to give me ten *chŏn* more at least. You're a
pretty good-sized man, you know. Heh, heh . . ."

"This is really ridiculous, trying to put the blame on
me! Listen, young man, since you put it that way, I
must tell you it was excruciating for a man of my size to
put up with your tiny rickshaw. In a car or a train, do
they charge passengers by weight? Have you ever heard
of that?"

"Heh, heh, but . . . "

"What's it going to be? Will you take this and go? Or
will you go without it? If you don't accept my offer, I'll
buy some meat with the money, mince it up, and have
it for my dinner."

"Just ten *chŏn* more, sir, that's all I'm asking. It can't
be worth all this fuss to you, not to a gentleman like
you!"

"Gentleman? If that's being a gentleman, I'd end in
ruin, all my property thrown away! Damn! If I run into
one more rickshawman like you, my days will be num-
bered!"

Had the rickshawman been at liberty to respond as
he wished, he would have told the old man that should
he run into another such customer, he would surely fall
in a dead faint.

Master Yun loosened his purse once more and took
out five *chŏn*. The thought that this additional cash was
a sheer gratuity irritated him, but faced with the persistent pleas of the rickshawman, he had no alternative
but to make it an earnest gift.

"This is ridiculous! Here! Twenty-five *chŏn* it is! You
can hang yourself with my belt, but you'll not get another *chŏn* out of me!"

Before Master Yun could finish speaking, the rickshawman took the three dull coins into his calloused palm, mumbled something indiscernible, whether expressing thanks or otherwise one could not tell, picked up the rickshaw shafts, and flew off like the wind.

"Damn! What a waste! Followed that bitch, had the misfortune to meet that bastard of a rickshawman, and the row with him has cost me five *chŏn*! That little bitch Ch'unsim came traipsing by, whispering in my ear about a Festival of Great Singers, and she coaxed me into going to the damned thing. . . ."

Out of sheer bad temper Master Yun was showering curses on Ch'unsim, but the accusation was entirely false. Why, his decision to attend the Festival of Great Singers in Pumin Hall had nothing whatever to do with Ch'unsim's desires. She simply boasted that her sister Unshim would be one of the accompanists at the festival. It had been Master Yun himself who had become all bright and sunny at the news.

He had persuaded Ch'unsim to accompany him, but not without repeated coaxing. . . .

The truth is, had it not been for the tip from Ch'unsim, Master Yun would never have gone to the Festival of Great Singers, and if he had found out the following day he had missed it, he would have been most grievously annoyed.

Getting a Free Ride: A Feat of Skill

Master Yun was greatly enamored of the Festival of Great Singers. With the exception of money, it was the thing he liked best in the whole world.

That Master Yun was born down in Chŏlla Province helps to explain his love of song; he was uncommonly enthralled by the sounds of the south. Since he loved music so much, he would have liked nothing better than to bring singing courtesans— kisaeng— and traveling troupes of mask dancers into his house three hundred and sixty-five days a year, but that would have cost an enormous sum. If he determined to do so every day for a year, perhaps a discount could be arranged by dealing with one of the kisaeng associations or the Korean Music Research Institute, but even then the expense would run to at least ten wŏn a day, three hundred a month, three thousand a year. . . . Whew! That was too much money for Master Yun even to think about spending. The proper term would be "an astronomical sum." Impossible even to contemplate.

Still, people everywhere have their own ways of surviving, and Master Yun found ways to quench these deep and seemingly unattainable longings: namely, the radio and the Festival of Great Singers. Master Yun was not entirely satisfied with these substitutes, but he took more than a little pleasure in them. And so he set up a little radio on the table next to where he slept. To Master Yun, this radio with three lights on its face was as precious as gold or jade. The sounds of the south wafted to him from the transmitters in the broadcasting studio. Lying comfortably on quilted cushions, the stem of his long pipe in his mouth, he listened constantly to the sweet music, muttering, "Good!" A pity indeed, he thought, not to be able to see the pretty faces of the girls or the gliding movements of the dancers, but it was still good.

The mission of keeping the radio tuned in to music programs was entrusted to Taebok, Master Yun's employee, whose numerous duties included servant, secretary, general factotum, and so forth.

On the days when Master Yun's favorite southern music, stylized traditional ballads, was not to be heard, thunder and lightning struck Taebok.

"Look, you eat three bowls of rice a day like everyone else. How can you be such an idiot? Why can't you tune in the music? It's played every day, isn't it?"

At such coldhearted rebukes, Taebok stood there speechless, scratching his head. The first few times, Taebok offered the excuse that programs were arranged by the radio station, and there was no law guaranteeing a constant supply of southern music, no matter how much you manipulated the dial.

Master Yun boiled over.

"Law? What the hell is this dogshit about law? You're only saying that because I called you an idiot. You're so sore at being called stupid you've got to blame somebody else, right? What goddamn kind of sound is it that comes out fine until last night and then suddenly today is cut off for no reason? That's what I say. Have all the *kisaeng* and the other performers dropped dead overnight?"

Mangled and battered like a cat caught eating from the dinner table, Taebok was the suffering target of these tirades. For some time the radio station had been receiving anonymous letters, dozens of them, all beseeching that southern music be broadcast every day. These anguished letters were dispatched by Taebok, who composed them in tears, literally, after bearing the full brunt of Master Yun's undue recriminations.

Master Yun's complaints, however, were not limited to these instances. If the music came on at all, it had to last at least two or three hours at a stretch. A miserable thirty-minute program— a blink of the eye which only teased the appetite— also irked him.

Even though Master Yun growled a bit from time to time, in his heart of hearts he was not displeased with the enjoyment he got out of the little box in exchange for what he had to pay: seventeen *wŏn* to buy the radio plus one *wŏn* per month in listening fees. Not at all a disagreeable investment, even to Master Yun. Nevertheless, when the time rolled around to pay the listening fee, he grew most reluctant to part with the money and raised his usual complaints about the radio:

"What do they think the damn thing is? Does it entitle them to shake me down for cash every month?"

Or he would utter, in a most unpleasant tone, "If that's the way they want it, tell them I'm cutting my subscription off from next month!"

At all events, such was the saga of the radio. Then, there was the Festival of Great Singers. The *kisaeng* and showmen came in all shapes and colors; and songs, too, came in all varieties. What is more, you could feast your eyes on the performers as long as you pleased. That the Festival, unlike that tease of a radio, was not always at hand was the only defect, but whenever it was held, Master Yun's pleasure was great indeed. In his mind, nothing would have been better than to stage the Festival of Great Singers every day of the year.

This Festival being the sweetest thing under heaven, every time it was staged in the vicinity of Seoul, Master Yun was sure to be there, even if the end of the world were at hand. And if ever he happened to miss a performance of the Festival, it was, of course, due to the negligence of Taebok.

Unless sent out of town on some errand, Taebok's daily routine included a visit to the barbershop at the corner of the alley to look over the newspaper, both to confirm the schedule of radio programs for the day and to check for stagings of the Festival of Great Singers, or for other performances sponsored by the Korean Music Research Institute.

If Taebok blundered and overlooked an event Master Yun wanted to be informed about, and if afterward it came to Master Yun's attention that he had missed a terrific spectacle, then Taebok was assailed with curses as thunderous as when he spent five *chŏn* too much by buying three cakes of bean curd instead of two.

Anyway, Master Yun so adored the Festival of Great Singers that on this day, even though the show was not set to begin until one in the afternoon, he was on his way out of the house before eleven-thirty, with Ch'unsim leading the way.

"What's the point of leaving so early? We'll be some sight, arriving there early and sitting by ourselves, staring at an empty stage," Ch'unsim said curtly, stopping short and turning back to Master Yun.

He grinned and stroking his whitish beard replied,

"You little bitch, there you go again, babbling like a little exorcist! Stop being difficult, now, and hurry on! Go on now, go on!"

After this gentle verbal nudge from Master Yun, Ch'unsim turned around and minced on.

The girl's face was oval, unlike a southerner's, and though hers was not exactly a rabbit face, her eyes were big and round, her nose sharp, and her lips full; the clear impression of the whole was a cute, bunny face. Yet offsetting her good looks was a frivolous disposition. Only fifteen years old, her face was not yet in full bloom, but due to the kind of life she had lived, the sights she had seen, and the sounds she had heard, her figure and carriage bore the imprint of a woman. Braided hair with a scarlet ribbon hung down to her hips, but if the truth be told, the pigtail was phony; it was tied onto her own bobbed hair. Her bangs, trimmed short and shriveled into artificial curls, were pinned up here and there. Her traditional blouse had been dyed pink and seemed far from new, but in combination with a long, colorful, pleated skirt, wrapped around her waist and casually tied with a man's necktie, the effect was altogether becoming. As for her face, there were signs of ringworm and fuzzy baby down on her skin still, and her powder was unevenly spread and smudged. Plop her down as is, and she would make a perfect addition to the innumerable young streetwalkers to be seen promenading along the stream by Kwanggyo Bridge. (But, please, do not think little of her because of this; currently she is in what you might call "love").

Ch'unsim had been mincing along in the lead for some time when suddenly she stopped, as if struck by an idea. She turned back once more and said, "Master!"

A series of sweet smiles flashed across her face. After

a few seconds of playfulness, she displayed an urgent restlessness.

"What are you up to now?"

"Since we're in such a hurry, let's take a taxi. What do you say?"

"A taxi?"

"Yes."

"All right, damn it."

Feeling a bit suspicious at Master Yun's quick assent, Ch'unsim carefully scanned the old man's face. Indeed, the broad grin he wore confirmed her suspicions.

"Do you really mean to go by car?"

"That's right, my little bitch."

"We'll find a phone and call one, then."

"No need to call, we'll get one a little ways on."

"Where? We'll have to walk all the way to Angukdong Rotary."

"There'll be one before then."

"There won't!"

"There will so! A huge, silvery car brightly shining . . ."

"You mean a bus, don't you?" Ch'unsim retorted sourly, cross at having been hoodwinked.

"You had a bus in mind the whole time, not a car!" she continued.

"Listen, little girl, it's no ordinary car, it's far more expensive than most!"

"You call five *chŏn* expensive?!"

"I wasn't referring to the fare, but to the cost of buying one."

Master Yun stood waiting with Ch'unsim at the bus stop at Chaedong Intersection. It wasn't the morning rush hour, but for some reason the first two buses were packed with passengers and passed by without stopping. Then a third pulled up, only slightly less crowded.

The two mercilessly thrust themselves on board, and the bus girl almost broke into tears.

Master Yun was totally unconcerned about the feelings of the other passengers, but he found it an ordeal to wedge himself into a crowded bus that was barely big enough to carry him alone. Besides, he had to bend over, taking up more space, lest his fine high hat get crumpled. Ch'unsim was trapped beneath Master Yun's armpit, and it seemed she might not have to pay her fare if he slightly adjusted the train of his coat to cover her.

When the bus finally reached the last stop in front of the Government-General Building, Master Yun and Ch'unsim got off with everyone else. All the passengers on the bus took a long look at the couple, as if to commemorate the occasion, before hurrying on their way.

Once off the bus, Master Yun heaved a sigh of relief and regained his composure. Only then did he slowly unfasten his purse and remove a ten-*wŏn* note.

"What do you expect me to do with this? I can't change it!" the bus girl grumbled angrily.

"What am I to do? It's money, isn't it?"

"Who said it isn't money? Pay in change!"

"I don't have any change!"

"There was a jingling sound in your purse just now, wasn't there? Don't try to . . ."

"Uhm . . . you mean this?"

Master Yun shook his purse, making the contents jingle, and then said, "This money is no good, counterfeit slugs. . . . Do you want bad money?"

He was about to unfasten his purse. The bus girl's face was all frowns.

"What am I supposed to do? How far are you going?"

"To the terminal."

"Then get change on the streetcar," the bus girl suggested.

"That's a good idea," Master Yun replied.

Presenting a ten-*wŏn* note when he had change in his purse, and falsely claiming to be going all the way to the terminal when he planned to get off at the Government-General Building— all this was premeditated.

Having successfully negotiated a free ride, Master Yun strolled at a leisurely pace from the Government-General Building to Pumin Hall, Ch'unsim leading the way.

"This is how I compensate for the inconvenience of riding on a crowded bus."

He took some pride in teaching Ch'unsim the feat of getting a free ride. Judging from this, Master Yun was not at all like the blue tile makers who are renowned for jealously guarding their trade secrets.

The Festival of Great Singers in the Countries of the West

A lot of time had been squandered en route, but the giant clock on top of Pumin Hall revealed it was barely noon as they reached the auditorium.

Even before the tickets were purchased, another big quarrel erupted between Ch'unsim and Master Yun. He insisted that since her sister would be performing, she ought to go backstage and find her sister to arrange for free admission. Ch'unsim, however, contended that despite her sister's position she had come with Master Yun as a respectable concertgoer, so she shouldn't have to go groveling for free admission. For a long while, both obstinately refused to yield. Then Master Yun nonchalantly took out two ten-*chŏn* coins and placed them in Ch'unsim's hand, in an attempt to soothe her.

"Here. Get yourself some roast chestnuts with this, and see about getting into the show for free. All right? That way, it's good for you and for me."

Even in the middle of summer, Master Yun was in the habit of referring to all money he dispensed to children as "roast chestnut money."

This twenty *chŏn* for roast chestnuts was enough to purchase Ch'unsim's scruples, and she made her way into the show by a backstage maneuver.

Master Yun quietly paid fifty *chŏn*, getting a red ticket for a cheap seat. This ticket in hand, he proceeded to the very first row by the stage and plopped down in the best seat in the house. Sure enough, the hall was deserted— he was the first to arrive.

After a short while, another early arrival, a gentleman in a Western suit who looked to be about forty, came in and selected a seat in the first row. For some reason, from the moment he sat down, the man in the Western suit kept peering at Master Yun with great interest. As if his curiosity was steadily mounting, he moved to a seat closer to Master Yun. Sitting there for a while, he seemed to be paying silent homage. He also looked most eager to strike up a conversation. Finally he spoke up, saying politely,

"It's getting tremendously popular, isn't it?"

Master Yun didn't know just what he meant by "popular" and, besides, he didn't feel like chattering with a stranger, so he answered unthinkingly, "Yes!"

The gentleman in the Western suit seemed disappointed with this response. After a while, he added,

"How much training is required to become such a famous singer?"

Finding the man an unseemly bother, Master Yun thoughtlessly replied, "Your guess is as good as mine."

"You're pulling my leg!"

"What do you mean, I'm pulling your leg? I'm a man who loves music, but I'm not a singer."

"There you go again! If the great Yi Tongbaek can't sing, who can?"

Could this be possible! How dare he mistake Master Yun for the showman Yi Tongbaek!

Master Yun felt angry and indignant at the unspeakable insult. Even today with decorum in such decline, had he been at home in Kyedong rather than here, Master Yun would have ordered this man thrown out of his house forthwith.

Master Yun, however, was a man who had weathered many storms in life— he had lived under the blade of the sword and more than once had peered down the muzzle of a gun. He was well aware, too, of the customs of the modern age and knew that to bark orders recklessly would only lead to his own disgrace. Choking back his rage, Master Yun showed the man the ticket in his hand to prove that he too had come to see the show.

Contrary to Master Yun's expectations, the man in the Western suit did not offer profuse apologies. He merely excused himself with a cursory nod in lieu of a bow. This impertinence, too, Master Yun resolved to endure, having already decided to suppress his anger. Just then another man in Western clothes showed up. It was a thoroughly luckless day for Master Yun. Judging from the artificial flower in his lapel, he appeared to be one of the ushers. While passing by, he had spotted Master Yun holding a red ticket while sitting in a white ticket seat. Had he not seen the red stub, it never would have occurred to him to suspect this dignified old man of such a ploy.

"Sir, these seats are for white ticket holders. Please move to the balcony," the usher in the Western suit requested in a gentle tone.

Master Yun was a bit mystified by this modern jargon — "white ticket seats"— and to be ordered to move upstairs was quite unexpected.

"Why are you telling me to go up there?"

"This area is white ticket seating, and since you bought a red ticket, your seat is up in the balcony."

"Why? This is a lower-class ticket! I paid fifty *chŏn* for this lower-class ticket! See for yourself!"

"That's exactly what I'm saying, sir. In your terms, this is high-class seating here. But you have a lower-class ticket, so I'm saying you need to move to a lower-class seat."

"Down here is high-class, you say? And up there is lower-class?"

"Yes sir."

"Now, see here. In heaven's name, what sort of rule is this? The higher place is lower-class and the lower high-class! I've never heard of such a thing in all my seventy years!"

"Still, that's the way it is. This is high-class, and up there is low-class."

"I never! Are we not in Korea? Is this a Western country? Is that why everything is turning topsy-turvy?"

"Everything modern is like that," the usher said with a laugh, "so, if you really mean to watch from here, why don't you pay one more *wŏn* to buy a white ticket?"

"That I cannot do! No matter what you say, to me this is a low-class place, so I'll sit here and watch!"

Faced with this superbly dressed man of enormous bulk acting like a spoiled child, the usher capitulated to Master Yun's infantile whining. In the end, Master Yun succeeded in viewing the show from a white ticket seat with his red ticket.

In fact, Master Yun thought it reasonable to assume the place was like a movie theater, where the ground-floor seats were cheaper. Based on several prior experiences, Master Yun knew the best seats for the Festival were those in the very front row next to the stage. From there, every move of the *kisaeng* and other performers was right before your eyes, every nuance in singing could be distinctly heard, and the ticket was cheaper because it was downstairs.

Armed with this esoteric knowledge, Master Yun had arrived intending to get a lower-class ticket for a seat up front, but it had turned out to be a white ticket seat that cost three times more. Whether you call it sheer obstinacy or unyielding tenacity, he prevailed over the usher and stayed put through the show. The best part was that, unlike when he sat up front in a moviehouse, where his cheap seat left him wedged in amidst devilish little imps who never failed to embarrass him by laughing at his girth, here today, to crown everything, his high-class low-class seat left him surrounded by aristocrats and pretty *kisaeng*, with nary an imp in sight.

Having relished the show, Master Yun sent Ch'unsim off home on foot, since she lived in Ch'ongjingdong. He walked alone to the streetcar terminal. But the prospect of boarding the streetcar along with the rest of the crowd swarming out from the hall, and the necessity of transferring to a bus, not to mention the breathless walk from Chaedong up that steep hill to Kyedong, was too overwhelming even to consider. He could have ridden free once more with that ten *wŏn* note, but suddenly the fear of heaven came over him, and a dreadful voice asked him why the hell he was being so stingy with money. Just at that moment he caught sight of a passing rickshaw, flagged it down, and consequently arrived at his front gate five *chŏn* poorer than he otherwise would have been.

The front gate was supposed to be kept securely locked, and the side gate was supposed to be bolted from the inside, but today the side gate was standing wide open. Whenever the front gate was left open, Master Yun couldn't help but feel his household property was leaking out and that ominous things were sneaking in. So he had commanded that the front gate be kept closed at all times, excepting only rare occasions when large loads of firewood or other merchandise were being delivered. Indeed, that the main gate should never be left open was a sternly enforced constitutional law in Master Yun's household, as the whole family knew.

Accordingly, the large front gate was kept sealed, and everyone coming and going, grown-ups and children, master and servants alike, had to make their way in and out through the small side gate. And that entrance, too, had to be kept closed, for to leave it open, as it was today, created the danger of inviting in unwelcome guests, beggars, and the like.

But of course, no matter how tough and relentless a beggar might be, not a coin was ever handed out. Still, such cases were most bothersome, for the intrusion had to be repulsed by argument. Consequently, whenever Master Yun spotted the side gate left open, a big scene always ensued. Thus today he was wondering who in the household had committed this egregious blunder.

An irate Master Yun, in no less agony than a camel traversing the eye of a needle, managed to squeeze through the side gate, slamming it violently as Samnam, one of the servant boys, dashed out to greet him.

A rather peculiar boy, this. In the first place, his hair was a sight to behold, curly and yellowish; and his head, resembling that of a half-wild calf, was so incredibly large it seemed to belong to someone else. His eyes were so severely crossed he had to turn sideways to look straight at anything, and his nose required its owner to hang his head during rainstorms. He was twenty years old, but the years must have rushed straight past him, for he looked not a day over ten. But to Master Yun, this boy was a cherished fool. As a rule, Master Yun never kept clever young boys as servants, the reason being that smart boys always ended up honing their skills at embezzlement.

Back when he still lived in the country, Master Yun had hired smart servants from time to time, but each such instance had resulted in a bitter lesson, for they invariably resorted to larceny. Samnam, the son of one of the caretakers of Master Yun's country estate, was generally reputed to be dull. Master Yun had taken him on a trial basis and, sure enough, he had turned out to be a priceless asset. He was very dense, and his extreme slowness could be irritating, but never once had he stolen so much as a match, not to mention his indifference to money. And being the son of a country ranger, he never asked for wages or other such nauseating things, unlike modern city brats. He was, to be sure, one of a kind, a truly matchless treasure.

Such being the situation, Master Yun normally would have uttered a nice "Yes!" at seeing Samnam rush out to greet him with a deep bow, but on this particular day he was so ill-tempered that whoever first appeared was sure to serve as a target for his thundering rage.

"Hey, you bastard! Who the hell left this gate wide open?"

"It wasn't me, sir! Mistress just came back, maybe she left it open."

The woman in question, Master Yun's daughter-in-law, was formally the lady of the house.

"I don't doubt it! Frigid bitch!"

Thus Master Yun cursed his daughter-in-law. This label, "frigid bitch," was for him a standard tag, sort of like a pronoun in a Western language. He always used it, whether the object of his curses was his daughter-in-law, his own daughter, a granddaughter, his dear departed wife, or his former concubine. As for men, he generally called them bastards whose balls should be cut off.

"The frigid bitch! Why does she have to be forever sauntering off on outings?"

"I don't know, sir!"

"Right. How could you know something I don't know myself? The frigid bitch! Her husband's been ignoring her, so she's in a frenzy, that's why."

"That's probably why!"

Regrettably, there was no audience to have a good laugh at this priceless scene.

Master Yun's constant swearing, even at his daughter-in-law's expense, was not just a case of an aristocratic foul mouth. Actually his honorable lineage was merely an appearance, like artificial silk or a gilded iron hairpin. Master Yun's ancestry was really quite pathetic.

Let Everyone Else Go to Hell

Master Yun's late father, Yun Yonggyu, whose nickname was "Horseface" because of his long horsy face, was not of noble blood. In fact, he lacked even the humble rank of a petty official in the county government. Nowadays, the fact that he had not even been qualified for a petty post is a matter of pride in the family. Back then, however, he was dying for any sort of low-level appointment, even a temporary one, but he just didn't have the education or the money to land one.

Until he was past thirty, Horseface Yun spent all his time loitering around the village gambling dens. He would sit there for hours, clad in humble peasant rags and a seamy big-brimmed hat, and whenever a big winner gave him a few coins, he set to gambling himself, joining a game of cards or a contest of darting birds.* If no money was forthcoming by these means, he sponged off his poor wife, who, hungry or not, worked as a seamstress to put food in the mouth of their little baby (none other than our Master Yun of today). Day and night he lazed about, sleeping away his life like the legendary So Daesŏng.* Horseface Yun spent half of his life in this sorry state. However, he was no coward. He

*See glossary.

was even somewhat valiant, but, of course, he was a
perfectly ignorant man.

One day Horseface Yun came into a "windfall." Out of
the blue, two hundred *nyang* fell into his hands, and
two hundred *nyang** in the countryside was as much as
two thousand in Seoul. In those days, the sum was
enough to make one a minor tycoon. The source of this
wealth was unclear: some said that he won it gambling;
others that his wife had inherited it from some distant
relatives; still others that the money was a gift from
goblins.

These days, whenever a poor man suddenly appears
to possess a large sum of money, our honorable police
officers make it their business to discover the source,
but this was more than sixty years ago; not a soul
uttered a suspicious word, even in passing. They simply accepted that the money must have been bestowed
by goblins, and, indeed, everyone was envious.

In any event, from that day on, Horseface Yun gave
up his habit of frequenting gambling dens. Instead, he
devoted himself to buying rice fields and to extending
credit, making short-term loans at fifty percent interest,
and longer-term loans at rates only slightly more philanthropic. Overnight he became a most industrious
head of household. The family fortune in due course
expanded like wildfire, as if he really had made a pact
with the devil. In his own lifetime, he grew so rich that
he was collecting over three thousand bags of rice from
his tenants every year.

From an early age his son Master Yun (then known
as "Toad Yun" due to his resemblance to that creature,
though his name was actually Yun Tusŏp), was very

*See glossary.

shrewd at usury. By the time he reached twenty, he had already demonstrated formidable managerial talents in assisting his father. In 1903, the Year of the Hare, he inherited all his father owned, and over the next thirty years he diligently devoted himself to multiplying the family fortune.

Ten years ago, when Master Yun moved with his family to Seoul, the records showed he was collecting annually ten thousand bags of rice in rents from his landholdings. Now, his capital on deposit in banks totaled about a hundred thousand *wǒn.* Judging from all this, Master Yun plainly belonged among those traditionally extolled sons who had excelled their sires.

In those dark days, accumulating wealth was far easier than it is today. Interest rates were ample and countless land titles were up for grabs. On the other hand, in the course of amassing such wealth in only two generations, father and son often had to endure unwarranted abuses by corrupt and greed-crazed county magistrates. Bound in stocks, they were beaten half to death; large chunks of the family holdings were confiscated; what is more, on numerous occasions they were held at gunpoint by bandits. Horseface Yun, in fact, met his untimely end at the hands of such thieves. When you think of it, the family had not come by its fortune easily— it was stained with blood.

Even now, whenever Master Yun thought back to those days, to his father's death, his heart pounded violently as vivid images returned of his father's body crumpling to the ground and of the grain-filled barn a blazing inferno.

March 15 in the Year of the Hare was unforgettable. March 15 was the day of his father's murder. Busy all day long lending and collecting money, dispensing rice loans in kind to the tenants who always crowded about during the hungry days of spring, attending his father's sickbed, such was the daily routine of Toad Yun, overseer of the family estates. After finally getting to sleep late that night, he had been awakened with a shake by his wife. At her urgent whispering, he instantly sprang to his feet. Not just once or twice, but scores of times he had been face-to-face with bandits, so even before he was fully awake, his body was steeling itself to the imminent peril. It was similar, perhaps, to the case of a general at the battlefront: though the mind sleeps, the body stays alert. At that time the Yun family spent their days and nights in uncertainty and anxiety. They could never relax, not even for a moment; they lived in constant fear and trepidation as if crossing thin ice.

The room was pitch black that night. Young Toad Yun sprang to his feet, gathered his pants at the waist without tying the belt string, and readied himself to bolt through the side door into the dimly moonlit night. He couldn't see his wife, but her labored breathing was in his ears, and when she fumbled forward to grab his arm he felt her hand shaking.

"Hurry! Now!"

His wife's desperate urgings were muffled by loud thumps at the main gate— it was being broken in with a wooden club or the butt of a rifle.

"Father! What about Father?" Toad Yun asked, freezing for a second in the posture of one about to bolt.

"I don't know . . . but . . . goodness, hurry! Now!" his wife answered.

She shook his arm, impatiently urging him on, but this push was unnecessary, for Toad Yun had quickly kicked the door open and was already gone.

Barefoot, without socks not to mention shoes, Toad

Yun sprang across the threshing yard in a single breath, crossed the wall, which stood as tall as a man, and moving as nimbly as if stepping over the threshold he dashed into the tall rye beyond. Once there, he dove down and began to crawl along the ground like a pheasant. Not more than five minutes had passed since his wife had awakened him.

In vaulting the wall Toad Yun had been unable to hold up his trousers, so now he was creeping stark naked in the rye furrows. Suddenly two shadows appeared around the far corner of the house. One held a rifle and the other a club. They were lookouts, charged with catching anyone who tried to flee over the back wall. It was undoubtedly a critical moment for Toad Yun. They hadn't spotted him running away and, unaware of their approach, he kept on crawling. Had they caught a glimpse of him, they would have given chase, and if he seemed to be escaping, they would have fired. But the two peasants, trained not with guns but with sickle and rake, might well have missed if they had shot their poker-like flintlocks at a man racing for his life through the dark reaches of the rye field. Once the naked Toad Yun had safely crossed the rye field, he emerged into a stand of pine trees. From there he sprinted all the way up the slope of the bush-spotted hill. Only then did he collapse in relief, totally out of breath.

On sensing the approach of bandits, the best tactic is to drop everything and run for your life without worrying about house and family. When bandits raid a village, they only apply the screws to the heads of households and other grown males. Whoever falls into their clutches is beaten half to death. The thrashing completed, all valuables are seized and carried off. One wrong move in the dreadful course of a raid could easily cost a man his life. Two, three— however many fall into the hands of the bandits— all are sure of the same fate.

This being so, every man for himself was regarded as the natural attitude. The first to realize the threat was at liberty to flee straightaway, without regard for the safety of parents or children. If a son, conscious of the peril to his father, attempted a defense, the assailants were greater in number and armed, and they cared as little for human life as for the life of a fly.

That night, therefore, Toad Yun had paused for a moment at the thought of his bedridden father, but as things were he could only save his own skin.

Horseface Yun, already sixty years old, had been released from jail only the day before. He had been flogged all over his backside, so for him flight was unthinkable. Calmly, he sat up in bed; he even lit the lamp. There was no avoiding this, and he still had guts enough to fight back out of sheer spite.

One of the bandits climbed over the wall and unbolted the gate. The others swarmed in.

"Don't let a single ant slip away!"

The bandit chief barked this order and then led the way into the detached sitting room wing of the house. Another cluster of bandits rushed into the inner quarters. The dogs, normally quick to bark and reputed in the neighborhood to be vicious, only whimpered, begging for their master's protection. You can judge from this the ferocity of bandits in those days.

"Don't lay a finger on the women or children!"

At this stern warning from the chief, the bandits heading inside responded in unison, "Yes sir!

This rule may seem unusual but it was enforced most strictly. The bandits who raided the house that night were a motley group— peasants in bamboo hats and cloth headbands, youths with their hair in long braids, wizened old men. However, this chaotic, ignorant rabble had never once, in their many atrocious raids, laid hands on women or children. If any one of them had, he would have been instantly beheaded by the bandit chief.

On entering the house, the chief had one of his men throw open the inner door. To his great surprise, he found himself face-to-face with Horseface Yun, who stared back at him with a venomous glare. For an instant the chief stopped dead in his tracks. He had supposed Old Man Yun would make a last ditch effort to escape. Never in his wildest dreams had he imagined the old man would sit there so boldly, as if to welcome him.

In the dim light of the oil lamp, the chalky, haggard face of the sick old man, peering murderously at the bandit chief, might have been that of a rancorous, white-haired ghost. Had he not had dozens of guns, rusty swords, axes, and clubs behind him, the chief, his heart chilled, might have retreated, step by faltering step.

Marshaling his nerve, the chief growled, "Well, well, so you're waiting, good!" This was not the first time that Horseface Yun had encountered this bandit chief and his pack. About a month before, they had raided the estate, stealing three hundred *nyang* in cash and more in promissory notes, and carrying off a cartload of goods and valuables. So these bandits were well-acquainted with the man of the house, and he, in turn, was very familiar with the chief's face.

Moreover, in the meantime there had been another harrowing incident that had left Horseface Yun so filled with hatred there was no room left for fear.

"Listen, Yun, you bastard, listen to me!"

The bandit chief scolded Old Man Yun in a menacing

voice, glaring down at him. The old man sat there rigidly, saying nothing.

"So you complained to the authorities and had my man captured! You expect to be safe after doing that? Admit it, you squealed, didn't you?"

"That's right. I went to the authorities and informed on you with my own mouth. What if I did?"

Fire flashed from the old man's eyes as he answered defiantly. He just sat there like a snake coiled to strike.

"So I informed on you," he continued. "What are you going to do about it? Hmmph! Thieving bastards, did you think you'd be safe plundering innocent people and living off your crimes? Sons o'bitches!"

The old man by now was shrieking in rage.

"You're the ringleader," he went on, "Wait and see, you'll be caught, too, soon enough! The day is coming when a blade'll kiss your neck, you bastard!"

The old man gnashed his teeth as he howled. It was the ultimate curse from a man with nothing left to lose. Come to think of it, it was a grand judgment on the old man's part. A confident sentencing of the oppressors, assured of their future punishment and of the ultimate victory of his cause. . . .

The old man, it's true, was ignorant, but he vaguely sensed that with the passage of time wealth would conquer the seat of power. His judgment had been a declaration of war, not only against the bandits, but against oppressors of all kinds, including the local authorities who were openly and recklessly indulging in blackmail. Whether the old man himself was conscious of this or not is beside the point.

"You pack of bastards! The night is dark and you think dawn won't break for a hundred years? Wait and see, you bastards!"

Old Man Yun went on like this in a bloodthirsty wail.

"Hah! You babbling old fool, that's only hollow talk! Hah!"

The chief feigned a laugh. Just then one of the servants who had been fast asleep on the far side of the room woke up, looked about in a stupor and immediately crawled back cowering into the corner. At the same moment, one of the bandits reemerged from the interior of the house and halted before the chief. A pair of white cotton trousers were hanging from the muzzle of his gun.

"The son got away, chief!"

"Got away? What have you there?"

"It's the skin the bastard shed when he jumped the wall. He must've woken up and run off without tying his belt and lost these on the way out."

Several of the men snickered under their breath, picturing the naked man running for his life.

"Imbeciles! How could you lose him?"

The chief clacked his tongue. Then he jutted his chin toward the servant quivering in the corner.

"Maybe you've been fooled and that bastard over there is the son."

Toad Yun hadn't been caught in the earlier raid, so the chief didn't know his face. One of the bandits took a closer look at the man in the corner and said,

"No, chief. This one's just a servant."

"Chtt. Nothing to be done, then. Just keep your eyes peeled. And don't touch a single spoon till I give the word!"

"Yes, sir! By the way, there's a cask of very good wine inside. Chickens and pigs, too, ready for slaughter."

Two years earlier, in the Year of the Ox, there had been a terrible famine, but even in a good year, bandit raiders were not likely to overlook meat and wine.

"Hear me well, Yun," the chief turned once more to threaten the old man. "You old bastard! The reason we've come is not so much for your possessions, but because we want to make use of you. So, what do you say? Will you do as we say or won't you?"

Old Yun had been gazing straight at the chief, but now he turned his head away.

"What'll it be? You refuse?"

"I won't listen to bandits! Would I do you a favor? I'd like to chop you up for food!"

From years of experience with bandits, Horseface Yun knew it made no difference whether he begged for mercy on his hands and knees or fought back, cursing them. In the end he would be robbed and beaten just the same. From the first, he knew how things would end, so he saw no reason to grovel. His hatred of this pack of bandits was so deep he really did want to eat them alive.

The night a month and a half earlier when the same gang had raided the family, Horseface Yun had recognized one of them as a man he knew well. It was a man named Pak, one of Yun's own tenants who lived nearby.

"Oh, you bastard! How dare you!"

It had never occurred to Yun that his tenants could hate him for the way he treated them. How could a ditch-digger living off my land join this pack of thieves and invade my house to rob me? The very thought made his heart burst with indignation and set his eyes ablaze.

When dawn broke the following day, Yun had hurried to the town center to see Paek Yŏnggyu, the county magistrate, who was an acquaintance (thanks to several prior episodes of extortion). Yun told him in great detail about the raid, saying that Pak so-and-so had been a member of the gang, and that if only they put the screws to Pak, then the whole pack of bandits could be apprehended.

Paek Yŏnggyu, however, went one step further. After hearing the whole story, Paek said he would bring in the bastard Pak, but he also said that since he was so knowledgeable about this bandit, Yun himself was under suspicion. The two of them would be questioned together, and Yun would be jailed for the time being.

When a cunning magistrate is determined to fabricate pretexts for blackmailing people, are there any bounds to unreason? A western king, Louis XIV I think it was, once thundered "L'etat c'est moi!" and in the Chosŏn dynasty, too, a certain member of the royal family, in the course of interrogating a prisoner from a warring faction, was said to have asked what sound a sparrow makes. The prisoner was to be executed if he answered "chirp"; if he answered "cheep" he was to be executed; and if his response was "chirp-cheep," he was to be executed just the same.

A county magistrate in those days was a virtual autocrat in his local domain. The most capricious whims had the force of law. And this particular official thought extortion of the rich a more interesting pastime than capturing bandits.

Having come in search of relief, Horseface Yun unexpectedly had had the tables turned on him; he was jailed. Pak was brought in and imprisoned that same day. The respective interrogations, however, were different. Pak was tortured to make him reveal the names of the bandits, their chief, and the location of their hideout. He confessed he had joined the bandits, but then he clammed up. His knee joints were laid open by leg screws, but not another word escaped his lips.

Meantime, Horseface Yun was questioned to extract a confession that he had been an accomplice of the gang, that he had harbored them and provided food and money. According to Pak's confession, Yun had made a pact with the bandits, and the magistrate declared that if Yun did not admit his complicity, he would be imprisoned and then beheaded. It goes without saying, the object of all this was blackmail. Without the least prompting from anyone, young Toad Yun immediately set to work, busily arranging bribes through back channels. One thousand *nyang,* in two five hundred-*nyang* bribes, was wolfed down by Magistrate Paek Yŏnggyu, and another thousand was spread around to fill the mouths of all the jailers, bailiffs, and other official retainers, high and low.

It took nearly a month and a half, and two thousand *nyang,* but Horseface Yun had finally been released the previous morning. After being beaten senseless, he couldn't walk and had to be carried home on a litter.

After this ordeal, Horseface Yun's vengeful hatred, aimed both at the magistrate and at the bandits, was boundless. Profound as this hatred was, the magistrate remained untouchable. As a practical matter, Yun's only outlet for revenge was the less formidable enemy, the bandits. And now the very same bandits had thrust themselves upon him, making all sorts of demands!

Horseface Yun's longing to pulverize and eat them alive was not unnatural; nor was it merely a narrow-minded reflex.

Pak's refusal to disgorge the location of the hideout or the names of his fellows, despite hideous torture, had been for the bandits a stroke of luck amid misfortune, so much so that the gang members were deeply touched by Pak's loyalty.

Putting aside for the moment the matter of seeking revenge against Horseface Yun, the first priority in the scheming of the bandits was to secure the release of Pak with the least possible risk. Were it not for this objective, they would have vanished quickly after finishing their work at Yun's house that night.

On finding a totally different Horseface Yun this time, a man inflamed with rage and stubbornly refusing to obey, the bandit chief was infuriated. "Are you serious?" the chief asked again, his eyes glaring ominously.

"Save your breath!" Yun said, undaunted.

"Don't be an obstinate fool!"

The chief stared at Yun for a time, breathing fire, then abruptly shifted to a soothing tone, admonishing the old man, "You'll do yourself no good this way. Cut the babbling and do as we say. Give three thousand *nyang* to those who have to be bribed. You bought your way out, didn't you? Isn't it only fair, then, that you buy the release of my man, a man you put in prison? There is no other way; you have to do it. I would rather do it myself, but I don't have three thousand lying around. To get that sum I'd have to rob ten bastards like you, and that'd take too long. Besides, I can't openly offer bribes myself, it'd be too dangerous. This can't wait; he's to be moved to the prison in a few days, I hear."

As he finished speaking, the chief's voice was almost imploring. He stood there awaiting Yun's reply. But Yun only sat there, his icy face turned away, pretending he had heard nothing. The chief, his anger surging again and his lips beginning to quiver, screamed,

"What'll it be? Yes or no?"

"No!" Yun shrieked back, uncowed.

"Do you think that I, a man praying for the arrest and execution of all you bastards, would use my money to buy freedom for one of you? Bah! The sky will fall first . . . No!"

"You mean it?"

"Yes!"

Old Yun was dead set. A beating at their dirty hands might be inescapable and they might be able to steal some of his property, but they couldn't dig up his rice fields and carry them away. Nor could they force him to throw away three thousand *nyang* to purchase Pak's release— such calculations as these underlay Yun's firm resolve.

"Are you sure?"

The chief tested Yun's intentions once more in a still more threatening voice.

"I'm sure! What can you do to me except kill me?"

"Drag him outside!"

Even before Yun finished his reply, the chief spun around and thundered the order to his men. Several of the bandits rushed over, seized Yun roughly and began dragging him out. At that instant, one of the inner doors burst open and in flew Horseface's old wife. Her white hair disheveled, she clung to him and wailed frantically.

The bandits were pushing Yun from behind and pulling him from the front, and though he struggled fiercely, they wrestled him to the threshold. In the confusion, Yun managed to grab ahold of the stock of one of the rifles. Once he had a firm grip on the gun, Yun no longer seemed a weak man. He summoned up all his strength, wedged the rifle against the threshold of the door, and planted both feet against the bottom of the wall. When they pulled his hair and pried at him with their wooden clubs, the old man moaned and groaned, but he wouldn't budge an inch. Unable to bear this spectacle any longer, the chief snatched a club from one of his men and with all his might aimed a blow at Yun's right hand, intending to break his grip on the rifle. In the flailing confusion at such close quarters, the blow missed its target.

Whack! Instead of hitting its mark, the blow hit Yun on the head with force enough to crack his skull.

"Aaachh!"

With one last cry, Yun crumpled to the floor, blood flowing from his head. His old wife's eyes bulged out.

"Aiieee! Now you're murderers, too. Kill me, too, you scum!" she shrieked, clutching the chief's arm and sinking her teeth into it.

Yun, sprawled unconscious on the floor, suddenly began to recover his senses. When the bandits started dragging him outside, Yun hadn't been sure of their intentions, except that they weren't good. It was only when, through the haze of pain, he heard his wife screech "Now, you're murderers, too," that Yun realized his death was at hand. He told himself that if he had to die at the hands of these bastards, he wouldn't go easily. He sprang to his feet, revived by the rage of desperation, snatched a sword, and began brandishing it about wildly. He grew still more frantic at seeing the bandits strike the old woman, something they had never done before. Yun hadn't seen his wife lock her teeth into the chief's arm; all he saw was the bandits flinging her away by the hair.

However desperately he waved the sword, the dying old man could do nothing against more than a dozen rifle butts, knives, clubs, and axes. When Yun fell, struck by an axe on the back of the neck, the chief's eyes burned with fire. He had never intended to kill the old man. Not that he wouldn't have dared to kill such a man, but he had planned to take him back to his hide-out. Like the mounted brigands who used to ravage Manchuria, the chief's idea had been to take Yun hostage and force his family to carry out their demands.

Eyes blazing, the chief stared for a while at the still body.

"Torch the barn and the grain!" he thundered.

Before long, huge flames rose from the outbuildings toward the night sky. Neighbors gathered and vainly tossed buckets of water on the fire. Only then did naked Toad Yun venture back to the house. By now, of course, the bandits were long gone.

Cradling his father's blood-soaked corpse, Toad Yun pounded on the ground and wailed,

"Will this stinking world never end?"

After calming himself a bit, he suddenly sprang up and, grinding his teeth, yelled,

"Very well! Let everyone else go to hell!"

It was a grand exclamation, indeed, and a great proclamation.

Such were the hardships in the early life of Toad Yun: Having learned how his wealth was amassed amid perilous storms, and finally dipped in blood, you won't find it unreasonable to see Master Yun trembling today at being parted from a single *chŏn.*

The particular ways and means employed for the accumulation of wealth were matters of indifference to Master Yun. In fact, were Master Yun tagged with the word "exploiter," he would have jumped high in the air in righteous indignation. By heaven, I'm a self-made man, he would protest. My money comes from industry and from a bit of luck in being in the right place at the right time—tenants, debtors, and grain-borrowers had nothing whatever to do with it.

When Master Yun looked back from the peace of the present to the old days of adversity, days reminiscent of, if not quite as earth-shaking as, the fall of the Bastille, he felt a great sense of relief. A complacent smile often crept onto his face as he sat there on his heap of wealth, of riches drenched in his father's blood.

True, they say a man on horseback is not satisfied till he has a footservant to stay the horse— that is human nature.

Times had changed, the old days of tumult were gone. In an age in which his wealth and safety were secure, Toad Yun, though he envied the riches of no one, had come to regret his lowly lineage. As a middle-aged man, indeed, he more than once had been plagued by "pistol men," sometimes known as "men in Western suits."

One such incident had occurred in December in the Year of the Monkey. On that day, a five-thousand-*p'yŏng* rice field Yun had long been coveting was about to fall into his lap. He was waiting at home for the seller to arrive and had four thousand *wŏn* in cash by his side. God knows how it happened— it continued to mystify Toad Yun for a long while after— but two men in finely cut Western suits walked into his house in broad daylight, sprang upon him, and took the entire four thousand *wŏn*.

Well, Toad Yun handed over the money without uttering even a grunt. That black hole at the tip of the cold iron gun barrel was inches away, pointed right at his heart— the Lord of the Underworld might as well have been looming right before his eyes.

In the old days, thieves only broke in at night. They had to smash the gate, so there was at least some warning, and maybe a chance to run away. But these characters came in broad daylight, arriving like well-heeled guests, and there was nothing you could do to escape their assaults.

On losing four thousand *wŏn* in this most ridiculous way, Toad Yun sat for a long while in a motionless stupor. After a time, his eyes came to rest on a piece of paper on the floor. They had left a receipt for the money.

"Huh! The world is so enlightened even the bandits have become civilized. They write you out a receipt after robbing you!"

For six whole days afterward, Toad Yun couldn't eat a bite or sleep a wink. The first two days were consumed by sheer longing for the lost money and the next four by worrying that the world might slip back into the old, bandit-ridden chaos.

These unwelcome guests paid several more visits subsequently, but they got no more money. After the first incident, Yun never kept cash at home, not even a ten-*wŏn* note.

A wealthy man living in the countryside was always being pestered with impost levies, calls for contributions, squeeze attempts by poor relatives, and worst of all, the constant dread of the strangers in Western suits. So in the end Toad Yun moved his entire family to Seoul.

When at long last the world settled down into a peaceful state, Toad Yun set out to improve the inferior status attached to his family ancestry. He laid down a four-point strategy for his lifelong mission to bestow distinction on his family.

First, he gilded his genealogy. Having dug up a few presentable names among departed distant relatives, he set up a temporary office and hired staff to draw up a new genealogical tree. So-and-so Yun, distant ancestor of Yun Tusŏp, was posthumously given the title of such-and-such minister; such-and-such judgeship went to so-and-so Yun; so-and-so Yun was a filial son; the wife of so-and-so Yun was a virtuous woman; and so on. In this way a decent-looking family tree was manufactured for him.

The job cost him about two thousand *wŏn*. Such a gilded genealogy was a snap to commission, but it didn't do much good, other than as an embellishment of the dear departed. Whenever he was introduced, he was still Toad Yun, son of Horseface Yun Yonggyu—Yun Tusŏp, son of the gambler Yun Yonggyu. As a result, he always felt there was a void where his esteemed ancestors should be, a gnawing emptiness like the hole in the stomach of a starving man.

Suppose you have a friend named Shin, and you constantly tease him because "shin" also refers to the monkey in the Chinese calendar. If that friend happens to find himself at a zoo, staring at a monkey, he cannot help wondering whether perhaps he is not a monkey after all. Similarly, suppose a man wanted to land a post as a rent collector or something, and in an attempt to flatter Toad Yun, went about reciting his freshly gilded genealogy from memory, referring to Toad Yun as "the honorable Yun Tusŏp, descendant of His Excellency, Minister So-and-so Yun," or as "descendant of His Honor Judge So-and-so Yun." In this way, the fabricated lineage would acquire a certain credibility, and Toad Yun himself would be greatly pleased. But then, clever and idle men of that sort are few and far between. One might as well set the genealogy to music, hire a pop singer to record it, and play it day in and day out on a gramophone.

The gains and losses from the genealogy business

were about even, and so the second step was for Toad Yun to get an official post for himself.

In the country, there was a school— *hyanggyo*— attached to the local Confucian shrine. At this school there was a public post dedicated to the worship of Confucius, Mencius, and other ancient sages. Each spring and autumn, the local folk killed a pig or an ox for a sacrificial feast. The *hyanggyo* was entrusted with these solemnities, and it was supported, monetarily and otherwise, by the local people. The elder who was head of the *hyanggyo* was addressed as "Master."

Traditionally, a *hyanggyo* master was a man elected by the local people for his command of the classics and his exemplary moral character.

In recent times, however, ever since the local government began administering the finances of the *hyanggyo* under its general affairs authority, the bureaucratic system had changed. A number of minor posts were established just below the rank of Master. Indeed, it seemed that anyone who made large tax payments, and who could afford to donate some land to these clerks or to retain their services on the side, could readily obtain the title of "Master."

Toad Yun, being who he was, could hardly hope to become a real nobleman, earning a high government rank as in the old days through the state examination. Neither would he have been satisfied with a position in the honor guard at the Royal Tombs. Though a bit disappointed with the level of the title, he condescended to procure the easily acquired magistracy at the *hyanggyo*, in this way becoming "Master Yun." Urged on by his dependents, he jumped at this chance to prefix an official title to his name.

For three years thereafter, Master Yun lived the life of

a master, presiding over the *hyanggyo* ceremonies in the spring and fall, his cues of "stand" and "bow" governing the rituals. He played the roles of aristocrat and scholar with diligence, extolling the great sages, the honorable Confucius and Mencius, and wondering which of the two was the stronger.

This riddle, whether the honorable Confucius or the honorable Mencius was the more powerful, was only one among the myriad of puzzles Master Yun created to stump the literati. This particular conundrum had its origin one summer day when Master Yun put in an appearance at the *hyanggyo.* Out of the blue, he posed this question to all the scholars assembled there: "Well, if the honorable Confucius arm-wrestled the honorable Mencius, who do you think would have won?"

The literati dropped their jaws, not knowing whether to laugh or to cry. Nobody was able to satisfy Master Yun's curiosity.

After three years of this magistracy, Master Yun resigned the position because of his move to Seoul. The esteemed title of "Master," however, as well as the riddle about Confucius and Mencius, were his for life.

The third point in Master Yun's strategy to embellish his family's status was the rather more brilliant enterprise of forging marriage links to the real aristocracy.

Master Yun's only son, Ch'angsik (strictly speaking, he was not an only son, for there was also an illegitimate son, but anyway) was of no help in this, for he was fast approaching fifty and already married to the daughter of a petty official in the countryside.

Master Yun had managed to marry his daughter into a certain family in Seoul of aristocratic descent. Unfortunately, this clan had fallen on hard times. The family barely had food to eat and lived in a squalid shack. To make matters worse, within a year after the wedding, Master Yun's son-in-law was run over by a streetcar, leaving his daughter a young widow. She was sent back to live in her father's house. Nevertheless, the marriage had forged a link to a family of rank.

In addition, Master Yun arranged a marriage between his oldest grandson and a girl belonging to the Pak clan of Ch'ungch'ŏng Province. Her family was also poor, but her noble ancestry was well recognized. His second grandson was matched with a daughter of the Cho clan. They lived in the vicinity of the Seoul Public Cemetery, but she was no daughter of a cabbage peddler, and if you traced the family tree back far enough, there was a cousin, thirty-seven or thirty-eight times removed, of Queen Dowager Cho, mother of King Hyŏnjong, the twenty-fourth king of the Chosŏn dynasty.

Thus, with three presentably aristocratic clans among his in-laws, Master Yun expected attention and deference when he cleared his throat.

The fourth and final point in Master Yun's strategy was the most important of all. It was to make members of his immediate family into men of real power and substance. A county magistrate, and a police chief. And, coincidentally, he had two grandsons. True, a provincial governor would have been better than a county magistrate and a police superintendent better than a chief, but then Master Yun thought it would be too greedy to want to run without walking first. Accordingly, he planned to begin by grooming the boys to be a magistrate and a police chief.

A Slum of the Heart

On his return from the Festival of Great Singers, Master Yun entered the house and, in the company of the witty Samnam, freely vented his accumulated anger by calling his daughter-in-law names behind her back. Only after unburdening his irritation in this way did he take off his hat and coat and enter the main room. He felt hungry.

A meal table was brought in by his second grand-daughter-in-law, Cho. With great care she placed it before Master Yun, who sat with his legs folded on a fancy mat in the middle of the room. Cho was the wife of Chonghak, the grandson slated to become a police chief, who at the time was studying law at a private university in Tokyo.

Born in Seoul, Cho had never been anywhere near a school, even though her family was supposed to have blood ties to Queen Dowager Cho. Her face was flat and covered with freckles, so that her general appearance was far from comely. To make matters still more lamentable, her face was marred by a lower lip which protruded as if it had been forcibly stretched. As if to make the most of this protruding lip, she excelled at glibly uttering the most unfortunate things. That her husband no longer paid her any attention and directed his interest elsewhere was due in part to that lower lip and to her habit of saying luckless things.

Ever since going to Tokyo to study, Chonghak had been sending letters home pestering his father to arrange a divorce. From Master Yun's point of view, however, this was just the babbling of the most ungrateful son on earth.

Anyhow, that is how the household came by its first grass widow.

After the meal table came a tray laden with a nickel-silver wine flagon and a cup, carried by the first granddaughter-in-law, Pak. She was the godsend of the household. Obedient and industrious, she was expert in the management of family affairs and knew how to humor the old man's whims. What more could be asked of her?

She had an oval face with big round eyes and at thirty looked younger than the other granddaughter-in-law, who was only twenty-five. Her only blemish, if blemish it was, was that her son, Kyŏngson, would be turning fifteen that year and there was no sign of a second son on the way. But then, a scarcity of sons ran in the Yun family.

Now, the situation of this woman was also dismal. In her case, there was no question of desertion or of her being the solitary keeper of the conjugal bedchamber, but her husband, Chongsu, Master Yun's eldest grandson, had gone down to the country estate where he lived with his concubine, so that, perforce, Pak found herself a de facto grass widow, though not through any fault of her own.

Under the four-point scheme Master Yun had laid out to embellish the family tree, Chongsu was being nurtured for a county magistracy. Six years earlier, therefore, he had left Seoul to take a clerkship in the government of the Yun's home county, taking with him his *kisaeng* concubine with whom he had established a separate family.

So, two grass widows . . .

Lifting the wine tray brought in by his first grand-daughter-in-law and warming it at the brazier in the upper corner of the room was Master Yun's daughter. Called "Seoul Mistress" by the granddaughters and servants, she was a genuine widow. It was she who had married into an impoverished noble family to further Master Yun's bid to forge aristocratic ties, only to be widowed when her husband was run down by a streetcar.

The appearance of this daughter— narrow forehead, wide-set eyebrows, flat nose, face covered with black sesame-seed spots, neck like a turtle's— matched her unhappy fate.

"You're so damn narrow-minded that young as you are you've already swallowed a husband."

Master Yun often shot such cruel words at his daughter. Whenever he said this, moreover, he never failed to tell himself that not only her narrow mind but also her looks were at fault. Having been brought up in affluence and never having experienced a pregnancy, she knew the agonies of a young widow, yet she was very immature for her age. She was twenty-eight.

Thus, there were two grass widows and one barrel widow who had never conceived a child. But this was not the grand total of widows in the family. Master Yun's daughter-in-law, Ko, was also a grass widow, you see. At the moment she was coiled up in her room across the hall, looking for an excuse to engage her father-in-law in an open clash.

And the family seamstress, who was from Chŏnju,

and so known as Chŏnju Taek, was another real widow.
A little earlier, Chŏnju Taek happened to be out in the
courtyard and she had overheard Master Yun berating
his daughter-in-law in vile language. Immediately she
had spilled this news to Ko, the tale being exaggerated
in the telling.

Consequently, the grand total of widows in the
household was five. Apart from a couple of servants,
every female in the house was a widow, so the calculation was simple enough, an easy head count.

This was a flourishing seedbed of widows, indeed. If
they were young plants in a nursery, one could wait for
transplanting season and distribute them to the neighbors. Pity was, these were human seedlings, and under
no circumstances could they be handed out.

After receiving his meal table, Master Yun scanned
the room with a searching glance.

"Where is T'aesik?" he asked.

The question was addressed to nobody in particular.
Of all the creatures in human form, the one Master Yun
treasured most was T'aesik, whose whereabouts he
now sought to determine.

T'aesik was fifteen, the same age as Master Yun's
great-grandson, yet he was Master Yun's son. The boy's
mother had not been Master Yun's wife — the child was
the fruit of a liaison with a winehouse woman down in
the country.

Whose belly had been borrowed was beside the point,
for when this child arrived, he was the apple of his
father's eye, naturally, because Master Yun was pushing sixty at the time. The child had been separated from
his mother within three days of birth and brought up
by a nanny under the scornful gaze of the whole family.
Thus, Master Yun felt sorry for the boy and rightfully

was more concerned about him than any of his other offspring.

Master Yun was in the habit of taking his meals in the company of T'aesik. This evening, with T'aesik nowhere to be seen, he refused to lift a spoon until the boy was located.

The two granddaughters-in-law, standing meekly in the cooler part of the room, had guilty looks on their faces. They feared a cascade of rebukes was in store for them. The Seoul Mistress seemed unbothered by her father's irritation. Approaching the table, wine flagon in hand, she remarked nonchalantly,

"I saw him playing out in the front yard just now."

"If he was out there just now, where has he run off to? Why isn't he here? If he leaves your sight, you should look for him before I ask you to . . ."

Sure enough, though Master Yun spoke to his daughter, the reproach was aimed at the entire household.

"That's easy for you to say; but how can we know every move he makes when he's running in and out all the time? He's fifteen now, and it's high time you stopped treating him like a baby!"

"Hummph! Suppose I turned my back on him as you say, it's not likely you'd care enough about him to see that he's fed regularly."

"You're so overprotective, always spoiling him. There's nothing left for us to do."

"A big talker you are, but wait and see what happens when I'm gone. He'll be out on the street with a tin can, begging."

"How can that be when you'll leave him an income of a thousand bags of rice in his own name? If someone who's left a thousand bags will be a beggar, whoever gets a mere four hundred will keel over and die!"

This bickering stemmed from the fact that Master Yun had set aside an estate paying rents of a thousand bags of rice to T'aesik, even though he was illegitimate and retarded, while his daughter's inheritance would only pay four hundred. At every opportunity she renewed her complaints about the injustice of this scheme.

While father and daughter were quarreling, the door of the room slowly opened and the boy in question stuck his head in to look about the room. The instant he spotted Master Yun, he leapt inside with a thump and hastened to plop down on Master Yun's massive knee.

In the course of this rumpus, T'aesik brought a frown to the face of the Seoul Mistress by knocking the wine flagon out of her hand. Although it hit Master Yun on the chin, he smiled broadly, rubbing T'aesik's head affectionately.

"Ha, ha, ha. Be careful now, Son," he said.

Judging from appearances, T'aesik and the servant boy, Samnam, might have been taken for brothers. Though T'aesik was fifteen, his body was no more developed than that of a four-year-old. Atop his tiny torso was perched a head so alarmingly large that his silhouette resembled that of a soybean sprout.

"Slow down a bit, son, what a fuss you're making. Now, look at this, look at this snot . . ."

A string of yellow-green snot moved in and out of the boy's nose with each breath, like a busily pumping piston.

"What is this, huh? If your nose is running, you should blow it or have somebody wipe it for you. Do you understand, T'aesik?"

Master Yun glanced at his daughter and granddaughters-in-law, and then he himself took two fingers and pulled the snot bar out of the boy's nose. The first granddaughter-in-law sensibly got a rag and stood in readiness before him.

"Dada!"

Having blown his nose, T'aesik raised his head and called for his father.

"Yes?"

"Me, many. . ."

He meant to say "money," but, playing the baby, he pouted his lips and out came "many."

"Money? Money again? I gave you some at lunchtime, didn't I? What did you do with that?"

"I bought sweets 'n ate them."

"You eat sweets all day long?"

"Give me mannieee!"

"All right, but save this until tomorrow and buy sweets then, all right?"

"Right."

Master Yun took a ten-*chŏn* coin from his purse. Upon receiving the money, the boy uttered a weird squeal peculiar to himself and jumped down from Master Yun's knee to sit beside the meal table.

Only after enjoying these shenanigans of his youngest son did Master Yun drink three cups of wine proffered by the Seoul Mistress. Meanwhile, T'aesik was beside himself, hovering over the table and picking with his fingers from every side dish. After eating he wiped his hands on his clothes, and the food he ate constantly dribbled from his mouth, but the Seoul Mistress dared not scold the boy in the presence of Master Yun. Her disapproval appeared only in the furrows on her forehead.

After finishing his three drinks, Master Yun lifted a

silver spoon inlaid with gold, and as he was about to take a spoonful of rice, he looked over abruptly at his two granddaughters-in-law.

"Why, you. . ."

There was an unmistakable tinge of displeasure in his voice. ". . . why don't you do as I tell you, huh?"

The two women had already grasped the problem and hung their heads contritely. Master Yun, seeing white rice before him, was rebuking them for not having mixed it with barley.

"Is all the barley gone already?"

"There's still some left," the first granddaughter-in-law answered diffidently.

"I don't doubt that. Why, then, did you cook only rice?"

He pressed the point, but no reply was forthcoming.

"Very well, it seems you pay no more attention to what I say than you do to the barking of the neighbor's dog. I keep telling you to mix a little barley into my rice, but you'd sooner die than listen. Tell me, why are you so dead set on eating pure white rice?"

"Please, Father, stop this poor-mouth nonsense," the Seoul Mistress said reprovingly, unable to bear the sermon any longer.

"Are you afraid, Father," she continued, "that eating a little white rice every day is going to drive a rich family into ruin overnight? The boiled barley ran out, that's why. So, stop this and eat your supper, please!"

"Does barley boil itself? What do you mean the boiled barley ran out? You've got to think ahead; boil some in advance and mix it with the rice for every meal! You're just making excuses. You're all so spoiled you don't want to eat any barley in your rice. Just excuses, I say. Go to a graveyard; will you find a single tombstone without an excuse?"

Master Yun put a precious spoonful of rice into his mouth.

Reflecting as he chewed, he thought it too precious to gulp down quickly; so he chewed it for a long time. Seeing that he considered pure white rice too good for himself, the thought that the whole household, maids and servants alike, was gobbling down this precious grain was too much to bear.

"You know, barley rice is supposed to be very nutritious. Barley gives a bit of texture and flavor to the rice, too. Why are you so dead set against eating it?"

There wasn't a sound, except for the noise of T'aesik gobbling rice. The granddaughters-in-law did their best to project expressions of unquestioning obedience.

"Besides, you don't even have to grind the barley in a mortar; I always have our country tenants grind it themselves. What's so difficult about boiling it— the firewood's always there— and blending a little with the rice? It's a mystery to me."

He paused for a moment, and then, altering his voice, began to speak very softly and sweetly.

"Children, there's another thing. You might not care much for barley rice, but if you eat it all the time, well, it can make a barren woman able to bear children. Children! Do you understand?"

He meant that even widows consigned to empty bedchambers might, if they religiously ate barley rice, become pregnant.

The impact of this assertion was tremendous. The first granddaughter-in-law was delighted, saying that if that was true, she'd eat barley without fail from the next morning. The second granddaughter-in-law, too, said that under the circumstances she might as well eat the stuff. As for the Seoul Mistress, even she thought the idea promising. Only daughter-in-law Ko, who was in her room across the hall seeking a pretext for a fight, thought the old man was up to his usual deceitful ploys and cast a dirty look in his general direction.

Ko always found the old man's conduct hateful. If she could have done so, nothing would have pleased her more than to yank him to the floor by his white beard. Yes, indeed, this woman Ko was one of the truly exemplary daughters-in-law in this world.

Like the old saying goes: "Bitch of a mother-in-law, if only a wolf would drag her off, the inner quarters would be mine, and so would her pipe." The coining of such a cruel old saying shows how hateful the species mother-in-law must be to the species daughter-in-law.

Ko had been wed at sixteen. Now she was forty-seven, and up to the day her mother-in-law died the previous January, for thirty-one long years she had lived a notoriously hard life under the heel of her mother-in-law. For more than three decades Master Yun's wife had supervised her every move. People called the old woman "wildcat" for her ferocity, "miser" for her stinginess, not to mention "nag" for her sheer contrariness. Many a tear of sorrow Ko had shed until the old woman's death the previous January finally freed her from oppression. She felt as slaves must feel at the hour of emancipation.

But then, this woman Ko hadn't been exactly an angelic daughter-in-law herself. True, an obedient and flawlessly virtuous daughter-in-law, once in the power of a ruthless mother-in-law, is only a mouse in front of a cat. But in Ko's case, although her character was as generous and well-rounded as her looks, she was also obstinate. Once her mind was set on something, nothing could budge her. She was very proud, as well. A physiognomist probably would attribute these character traits to her endomorphic constitution. Anyway, through thirty-one trouble-ridden years under the roof of her parents-in-law, Ko had borne the burdens of an unusually large household without succumbing to the disaster of being kicked out.

In the meantime, she gave birth to two sons, Chonghak and Chongsu, furnishing Master Yun with the stock to cultivate a county magistrate and a police chief. And now, nearing the age of fifty, her hair half-gray, she even had a grandson in the second year of middle school.

Then, in January of the previous year, her mother-in-law, wildcat or lapdog, departed this world, dragged off not by a wolf but by diabetes. With the role of mistress of the household falling vacant, it would have been reasonable for daughter-in-law Ko to take charge, even though she had no use for the old woman's pipe since she smoked cigarettes.

A mother-in-law is supposed to love her son-in-law even if he is pock-marked, and a father-in-law is supposed to love his daughter-in-law even if she has buck-teeth and one eye, but Master Yun, for some inexplicable reason, outdid his wife in hating Ko.

Once the old woman's funeral and the associated formalities were over, it was time for the Seoul Mistress, sad though she might be, to move out of the mother-in-law's large room in favor of her sister-in-law, Ko. But Master Yun intervened, saying, "Listen, dear! As you know, I always eat my meals in this room. If you make this your room, how can I use it in comfort? So till I die, you'd better stay in the room across the hall."

This had a certain plausibility, of course. So, after

the mother-in-law's corpse was taken away, the large chamber was shared by the Seoul Mistress and T'aesik, and Ko had to keep to her old room as before. Whenever she reflected resentfully on this business of living quarters, she never failed to tell herself,

"Humph! A worthless woman isn't allowed to watch an exorcism on her own husband; I'm doomed to a servant's life until my legs go stiff."

Denial of her claim to the larger room was not the only wrong Ko felt she had suffered. On her deathbed her mother-in-law had gasped her hatred for her daughter-in-law.

"Yes, I know who loathes and detests me most. Now that I'm dying, I see there'll be someone singing and dancing for joy!"

Obviously, this was targeted at Ko. The thought that her departure would leave Ko as mistress of the family, doing everything as she pleased, was so unbearable to the hateful old woman that she uttered these icy words with her last breath.

Ko in fact did recover her high spirits from the moment she donned mourning clothes. Examples could be multiplied indefinitely, but to take only one, she knew that the sound of a match being struck in her room late at night would no longer lead to a scene the next morning. The old woman could no longer thunder "Who the hell was smoking all night? There must have been seventeen matches struck!"

With the old lady gone, Ko was now at liberty to spend her sleepless nights in the uninhibited company of cigarettes. And nobody would nail the door of her room shut if she left the house for an outing.

Except for a little more freedom in her daily life, however, no substantial changes took place. Ko's father-in-law, Master Yun, had shunted her aside, even though she was rightfully entitled to inherit the supervision of the household, and, skipping a generation, he had bestowed that power on the elder granddaughter-in-law. In other words, Ko's own daughter-in-law, the wife of Chongsu, had succeeded Master Yun's wife and had now been put in charge of all the affairs of the family.

Ko had taken it for granted that she herself would be the boss, with her daughter-in-law taking orders from her. But she had been passed over like an acorn in a dog's food, and life would go on under her daughter-in-law as it had under her mother-in-law. Her predicament was not unlike that of one who succeeds to the throne on the death of a monarch, but finds all real power has fallen into the hands of a younger prince.

To make matters worse, as time went on Master Yun's growling complaints against her became simply unbearable, as though he was making up for his dead wife's absence. The Seoul Mistress, too, once ensconced in the disputed main bedroom, started playing the role of queen, finding fault with every trifle that transpired in the house. As if these weren't enough, there was yet another, bigger problem that fed the fire of anger in her heart.

Ever since Ko had given birth to her second son, Chonghak, who was presently in Tokyo studying to become a police chief, all marital relations with her husband, Ch'angsik, had been severed. She had wasted the next twenty-four years, the prime of her life, in grass widowhood.

Ko's husband had taken a concubine while still in the country and set up a separate household with her. When they came to Seoul, he brought her along and set up a second house near Tongdaemun. More recently, he had hooked up with a third woman, a *kisaeng,* something he had seldom done in the past. Of late he was keeping this second concubine in yet another house in Kwanch'ŏldong. He now split his time between the two, sleeping at one house and playing at the other.

The only occasions upon which Yun Ch'angsik was forced to visit his father's house were when he needed money or when he had to respond to a persistent summons from Master Yun. Even then, he only met his father in the outer reception room. He never entered the inner quarters.

The personality of this man was totally different from that of his father. There was a world of difference, too, between this Mr. Yun and his nagging wildcat of a mother. He had an unassuming devil-may-care way about him that he seemed to have inherited from his old grandfather, Horseface Yun. He was forty-six years old, and since reaching the age of discretion he had never raised his voice in argument with anyone. If people treated him badly, instead of pressing the point, he ignored them. But then, he was so good-natured he very seldom made enemies. He didn't concern himself with the family fortune and, indeed, was not at all competent in managing business matters. According to his father, he was an ignoramus, nearly fifty years old, who had never developed any practical sense—a man as utterly oblivious to the progress of worldly affairs as he was to family interests.

This description was not entirely unfounded, if one were intent on criticizing him, but on the other hand, some might view him as a man who was above material avarice.

Whenever a friend or poor relative appeared on his doorstep with a tale of hardship, Ch'angsik never refused help. Immediately he handed over what money he had at the moment. He frequently acted as guarantor for his friends and often ended up with creditors enforcing those debts against himself. On several such occasions, when his son faced execution of judgments in amounts over ten thousand *wŏn,* Master Yun obtained court rulings that his son was a quasi incompetent for whom the father was not legally responsible. These steps, however, didn't stop the son, for as soon as he was adjudged a quasi incompetent spendthrift, he simply forged a seal bearing his father's name and went on borrowing and guaranteeing as he pleased. Plenty of people were willing to discount tens of thousands in commercial paper as long as they bore the seal "Yun Ch'angsik, son of Yun Tusŏp," even though the seal was known to be forged. Later, when the paper came due, Master Yun couldn't very well let his own son be jailed as a forger, so he had to pay the bill or note.

Being a man of this sort, Mister Yun Ch'angsik's life had settled into a predictable routine. He went out drinking with friends, practiced archery, took seasonal tours to the most scenic places, collected ancient Chinese books, contributed classical verse to a newspaper, drank at one concubine's house until he got bored, moved to the other concubine's house for a game of mahjong, and so on and so forth. In short, his life was so free of earthly cares that in some ways he seemed an otherworldly being. Of course, witnessing his nightly comings and goings, his dalliance with concubines, his bouts of mahjong and visits to *kisaeng* houses, one might have taken him for a dissolute scoundrel, a common reprobate.

Fate allots eccentricities to each of us, it seems, and Yun Ch'angsik was no exception. A certain notable in the field of education once knocked at his door, having learned by hearsay that Mr. Yun was too generous to deny requests for donations. This influential gentleman told a story about how a private school he supported was in financial distress of late and how he was searching for a patron in a position to donate about two hundred thousand *wŏn,* which, along with capital raised from other sources, would be used to restore the school to a firm financial footing. So, he went on, wouldn't Mr. Yun be kind enough to donate one hundred thousand or two hundred thousand to this deserving cause?

The visitor delivered a long and eloquent oration in an attempt to sell Yun on the idea. Throughout the speech, Mr. Yun kept saying "Oh, is that so?" and "Sure, sure, I understand," agreeing with his visitor, but when the time came for him to answer, he said, "That people can't go to school is not because there aren't enough schools, but because the students don't have the money, isn't that so?"

At this unexpected query, the notable was crestfallen. After exchanging a few more words, he left.

As a matter of fact, Yun stood ready to help out friends and acquaintances in need, but never in his life did he spend a single coin on public charities or philanthropic causes.

His father, Master Yun, on the other hand, frequently made charitable contributions. When they lived in the country, Master Yun had underwritten the entire cost of constructing a martial arts hall for the local police station. He also made two gifts of fifty and one hundred *wŏn* to the fire department. Once he even donated two hundred *wŏn* to defray the expense of expanding a primary school classroom. When a disastrous flood hit South Kyongsang Province, he bought a piggy bank and filled it with coins in the amount of one *wŏn,* seventy-two *chŏn.* This bank he gave to T'aesik and sent him with it to a newspaper company which was collecting money for the flood victims. This donation was deemed to merit a photo in the same newspaper, and that photograph had become a treasured family heirloom.

Under no circumstances, however, would Yun Ch'angsik have undertaken such initiatives. If seriously beleaguered, he might put an end to the pestering by referring the supplicant to his father, but never would he make a donation of any kind himself.

There's an old saying that the rich sooner or later get no richer. What this means is that if it takes a million or ten million to make a man rich, from that point on he will hover around that level of wealth, a little more or a little less— his fortune cannot keep snowballing.

As a matter of fact, there's truth in this saying. Take Master Yun, for example. It had been over ten years since his annual income reached the level of ten thousand bags of rice. That converts into about one hundred thousand *wŏn* per year. In addition, he earned another twenty or thirty thousand yearly in interest from lending and trafficking in bills, notes, and other commercial paper. His annual income, then, hovered somewhere over one hundred thousand *wŏn*— nothing to sneer at, eh? Now, all the taxes payable plus living expenses wouldn't have exceeded fifty or sixty thousand *wŏn*, far less than his income. One would suppose that a man who had already been a millionaire ten years earlier would have increased his fortune by at least half over a decade.

For all his eagerness to enhance the family fortune, however, Master Yun's income ten years later remained around ten thousand bags of rice per year. This certainly was not due to any indifference toward capital accumulation on the part of Master Yun. His son Ch'angsik had been squandering money right and left, and the debauchery of his first grandson, Chongsu, consumed more money, not to mention the graft to further his quest for a county magistracy. Under these circumstances, the family fortune had hit a ceiling at ten thousand bags of rice annually.

Sometimes, when he had to settle the debts of Ch'angsik, Master Yun exploded in rage. Summoning his son on such occasions, the old man seemed ready to execute him on the spot. Ch'angsik never appeared at the first summons, however. Only after three or four messages would he reluctantly turn up.

As long as he was alone, Master Yun just simmered, but at the sight of his son nonchalantly sauntering in as if nothing had happened, his heart instantly swelled to the bursting point and an avalanche of curses rolled from his mouth.

"You bastard, I'll have your balls cut off!"

Ch'angsik replied with a gentle rebuke,

"What a thing to say, Father. Why, your grandsons are all grown up, and Kyŏngson would be old enough to marry if this were the old days, so how can you talk that way . . ."

"What . . . what's this?"

Master Yun was speechless. His son always reprimanded him for his foul mouth, but the old man felt no remorse for his swearing. For some reason, however, Master Yun felt restrained by his son's presence.

On his own, of course, Master Yun would be firmly determined to give the bastard a merciless tongue-lashing, but once face-to-face with his son, he was the one who felt defensive, and all his angry designs came to naught.

"Nothing under the sun scares me as much as that bastard. He's worse than a tiger or a bandit," Master Yun invariably would say of his awful son.

That Master Yun, who feared nothing else in the world, was petrified by Ch'angsik was not because of menacing strength or withering eloquence, but simply because of a certain air, subtle yet overwhelming, he had about him. This uncanny power to immobilize his father was what made Ch'angsik more fearsome than a cutthroat or a wild animal.

Always disarmed in this way, all Master Yun ever managed to say was, "Pay back my money, you bastard! The money I used to pay off your debts!"

"Please deduct it from my share of the inheritance," Ch'angsik, perfectly composed, would reply.

"Get out of my sight before I have your balls cut off!" Master Yun would screech breathlessly, turning his back on his son.

Without fail, Master Yun ended the loser in these battles. Yet he had to fight at least once, sometimes twice or even three times every month. These battles over debts were not only with Ch'angsik, but also occasionally with his first grandson, Chongsu. Ungodly ordeals they must have been for the old man.

Besides these sorts of quarrels, from time to time clashes unavoidably erupted between Master Yun and his daughter, the Seoul Mistress. There were fights with his second granddaughter-in-law, as well, and with her husband, Chonghak, whenever he came home from Tokyo during college vacations. Needless to say, there were also battles with his daughter-in-law Ko, and sometimes even fights with the servants, Taebok and Samnam, were unavoidable.

While the head of the household constantly engaged

in such battles, Kyongson fought with T'aesik. And the Seoul mistress fought with Ko, with her nieces-in-law, with Kyŏngson, and with T'aesik, besides fighting with Master Yun. Ko, meanwhile, battled not only with her father-in-law, but with her daughters-in-law, with her sister-in-law, and with her sons, whenever they came home. She also sometimes rushed off to the houses of her husband's concubines in Tongdaemun and Kwanch'ŏldong, picking fights and smashing things.

Fight, fight, fight— the whole Yun clan seemed ready to fight at the drop of a hat. It seemed they had all pledged to make fighting their remedy of first resort. And on this particular day, a battle was about to break out at any moment between Master Yun and Ko.

Reports from the Front Line

After long years of sleeping alone, Ko had finally left behind the age of childbearing, passing the threshold at which a woman is a woman no longer. On reaching this stage, even a woman who had been leading a harmonious married life begins, it is said, to exhibit mysterious symptoms of illness— hysteria, for instance. Ko, having wasted twenty-five years in utter solitude and now about to part with her womanhood forever, understandably was filled with rancor. To make matters worse, she had been deprived of the joy of taking charge of the household. And her sons, all grown up now and living far away, never seemed to give their mother a thought. As for her grandson, Kyŏngson, she found him anything but cute; he was detestably spoiled and always provoking her. Her husband was at best a stranger, if not a mortal enemy, and the old man, her so-called father-in-law, was always ready to eat her alive for no apparent reason, raining curses of the vilest kind on her. From Ko's point of view, therefore, her spiteful and ill-tempered demeanor seemed only natural.

Until her mother-in-law's death the previous January, Ko had been able to bottle up her complaints inside her. This was sheer force of habit after thirty years of being a mouse in a cat's domain. When the tyrant vanished, Ko soon recovered her full vitality. Yet the world still refused to revolve as she desired so that her complaints now were transformed into a fiercely cantankerous rancor. With the demise of the old witch, the only member of the household older than she was Master Yun himself. Everyone else was below her. As far as Ko was concerned, Master Yun was a senile old fool. She had no more intention of according him the deference due a father-in-law than she had of kowtowing to any other doddering old relic in the neighborhood.

In this belligerent state of mind, Ko was intent on joining battle with anyone in the family, regardless of age, on the slightest pretext. This evening was no exception. She had resolved to blow her top in order to repay Master Yun for the undeserved curses poured upon her for having left the side gate open.

But if the truth be told, that gate had been left open deliberately— precisely because Master Yun was sure to be angered at the sight of it. And when, as expected, the old man responded with a torrent of abuse, she was ready to accept the invitation to duel. Like the legendary serpent who grew ill-tempered after being deemed unworthy of metamorphosis into a dragon, Ko had reached a point where the only pleasure in her life was to fume in her room, venting her inexhaustible rancor.

She was hungry for a row to cool her rage, but as she eavesdropped on the goings-on across the hall, all she heard was the old man filling the ears of his granddaughters-in-law with deceitful nonsense about barley rice being an aid to childbearing. No foul language was being spewed her way. If she controlled herself and said nothing, her rage would just grow. Besides, she had no one to fear and there was nothing to stop her, so why, she asked herself, should she be careful, why should she choke down her anger? By this time her cheeks were drooping, in crude terms, like a horse's you-know-what on a hot summer day. She was extremely agitated and panting hard, with nostrils flaring and lips twisted into a pout. Repeatedly, she pulled her knees to her chest with locked hands, then stretched her legs out again. She would light a cigarette, quickly stub it out, and relight it once more. In truth, a person who longs to fight but cannot becomes doubly enraged.

Everyone was cautious, not even daring to cough, and the whole house was dead quiet, except for the muttering sounds from the young boy.

Outside, the twilight was quietly deepening. The lights came on in the half-dark room like a sudden dawn. Just then, as if the light had been some sort of signal, there was a loud clatter of footsteps at the gate and Kyŏngson walked in through the front yard, shattering the wary silence of the house. He seemed to have just come from school, judging from his uniform and the bookbag on his back. But at the sight of his great-grandfather's shoes in front of the wooden floor, the boy stopped short, retracted his head like a turtle, stuck out his tongue and whirled around, heading on tiptoe into the back precincts of the house.

Kyŏngson was taking precautions in advance, for he knew only too well that no welcome awaited him— the chances were he would be greeted with a scolding for having teased T'aesik to tears a few days before.

Kyŏngson was sure nobody had seen him, but his grandmother, Ko, had her eyes fixed upon him. She couldn't care less if the boy attacked the old man. Her reason for shouting at him was not because she saw his tongue dart out in Master Yun's direction; she just meant to use the boy to pick a fight.

"Kyŏngson, you little bastard!" she yelled in a voice loud enough to shake the whole house, her verbal thunderbolt almost cracking the windows. Everyone in the house was, of course, startled out of their wits. Kyŏngson lurched backward in shock. It was quite unexpected that the attack came not from his great-grandfather but from his grandmother, who seldom had anything to do with him. The boy's surprise was unbounded.

The shock wore off after a moment, however. Kyŏngson recovered his composure, turned around slowly, and calmly looked straight into his grandmother's face.

"Yes?"

While the old lady burned with fury, a murderous light shooting from her eyes, the boy was quite cool and collected. He didn't even blink— his self-composure was such that the beholder might well have been tempted to skin him alive.

Having failed to find a pretext for fighting with her father-in-law, Ko had decided to grab anyone passing by, whip up enough of a ruckus to get on the old man's nerves, and then, if he began to curse, she would use this as a pretext to start a fight. The insolence of Kyŏngson, the little bastard, threw her into yet greater rage, but deep down she welcomed this further incitement of her fury.

Kyŏngson, on the other hand, was not in the least scared. Even though everyone in the household was his senior, to him none of them was worthy of being considered human. Thus, he feared no one, and nothing anyone said could intimidate him.

Kyŏngson looked down on all of them; they were nonentities— his great-grandfather Master Yun fell into this category, as did the Seoul Mistress, his grand-aunt; his grand uncle T'aesik didn't even count; and as for his own father, Chongsu, his aunt, Cho, and the concubines of his grandfather, Yun Ch'angsik, they were all nobodies.

Kyŏngson sized up the situation rather astutely. Bah, he said to himself, she must be having one of her usual fits! What a sight she is! She can go right ahead; see if I let her make me the scapegoat of her evil temper.

As though she might do something outrageous at any moment, Ko kept screeching, "You little bastard! You little bastard!"

All she could do was repeat the outburst; she had no reprimand to level at him.

Still, if a mere daughter-in-law dared be so impertinent as to create a commotion, shouting and slamming her door shut, thus to disturb her father-in-law at his dinner, the old man would be sure to find such behavior deplorable and a declaration of war would inexorably follow. And this is exactly what Ko was aiming at.

First, however, Ko had to deal with Kyŏngson, who stood defiantly before her, as if to say, why are you squealing like that? Out with it, if you have anything to say! Never saw such a sight in my life!

Ko found his snide attitude unpardonable, but as the one who had created the scene, she had to finish it off to save face, to salvage the dignity befitting an adult.

"You bastard! Where have you been? What have you been doing? What do you mean showing up here at this hour?"

This was the best she could come up with.

Ordinarily, she would have been quite unconcerned about whether her grandson was on time going to and from school and indifferent to the diligence he displayed in his studies. The ulterior motive for this out-of-character remark on this particular night was rather obvious, but Kyŏngson had to save his neck by producing some plausible excuse.

"We were getting ready for an exhibition at school! That's why I'm late!"

His answer was immediate, but the tone of his voice was full of undisguised resentment and scorn. His mother ran in hurriedly from the main room, and in a gesture of respect to her mother-in-law, quietly joined in the scolding of her son:

"You should've come straight home after school. Where've you been wandering? . . . it's very late . . . you shouldn't make your grandmother worry about you."

"What do you know, anyway, Mother?" Kyŏngson snapped back at his mother in an irritated voice, but his reproach was really aimed at his grandmother.

"I said I had to stay late to work on the exhibition, didn't I? None of you know anything about it, so why don't you just shut up?"

"Why, you nasty little bastard!"

"Be quiet, Mother. . . . What do women know about anything, sitting in the house all day? Just because I'm the youngest, everybody in the house picks on me whenever they're angry. But why should I take it? Why? I may be young, but I'm the one who'll be head of this family before long. . . . Everybody is quick to jump on my back . . . I'm fed up!"

Kyŏngson poured out his prepared reply smoothly, without a hitch.

"How dare you!"

His mother, unable to muzzle her son with feeble recriminations, was about to rush over and smack him. But Kyŏngson ignored her and went stamping off toward the back of the house.

"Humph! Some bloody family we have!"

Disgusted by the ludicrousness of the scene, Ko closed her door with a bang and went on with her aimless ranting.

"A nice example, I say! A little bastard still wet behind his ears, howling like a rabid dog at the slightest rebuke from a grown-up! No wonder! No seed worth anything ever sprouted in this family!"

No sooner had Ko dropped this curse, impugning the whole family tree, than Master Yun thrust the door wide open, ready to square off for a fight. By God, wasn't he mad!

Actually, Master Yun was not unaware of Ko's intent, but he had been curious to see how far she would go, so he had waited. That was why he made no move when Ko first started yelping. Instead, he just glanced over at his daughter and his granddaughters-in-law.

"That frigid bitch! What's she raving about this time?" he said, lips quivering.

The Seoul Mistress twitched her lips like her father. The two granddaughters-in-law silently hung their heads for a time, then the first slipped out alone to the hall to reprimand her son. And T'aesik, upon noticing Kyŏngson's return, went over to the sliding glass window to look outside, then came back to his father and stammered,

"Dada! Dada! That Kyŏngson, right? So bad, yeh, bloody bastard, yeh?"

"Now, now, where did you learn such. . ."

"Wha? Dada, Kyŏngson's a stingy bastard, a thieving bastard, yeh? Right, Dada?"

"Now, now, I won't have you using such language!"

But Master Yun was beaming with delight at the verbal facility of his little son, and the scolding was not in earnest.

Even when Master Yun heard Ko yelling again at the top of her voice, he merely glanced over at his daughter and second granddaughter-in-law in turn, muttering the same maledictions he habitually leveled at Ko, such as, "The bitch is having another fit," "She's ranting because her husband left her for another woman," or "She was born into a low family and never learned any decency, that's her problem".

Meantime, Ko's bellicose mood had ripened to the point where she had at last cursed the whole clan, ancestors and all, stigmatizing the entire family, past and present, as subhuman.

Master Yun was not about to exhibit indulgence. Such an attack could not be permitted to pass unchallenged; he decided to join battle, showing no lenience.

"Listen here!"

The sliding door was thrust open with a deafening noise and Master Yun approached the hall. His spoon had already been flung away, striking hard on the corner of the meal table.

"Just what's so great about you! What on earth have you done that's so good? Tell me, open that manhole of a mouth of yours. Speak up! Let's hear it!"

His voice by this time was loud enough to shake the rafters. It was a voluble voice even when he wasn't agitated because he was a good-sized man.

This was the opening for which Ko had been hoping.

"I've done nothing wrong! Not a fly has cause to complain about me! It was my rotten fate to marry into this loathsome family, and that's the only sin I've ever committed! Why are you always growling at me, as though you wanted to eat me alive? Is that my reward for the thirty years I've been serving you? Because I'm fat, do I whet your appetite for meat? I'm sick and tired of this! It disgusts me!"

Intentionally or not, a certain etiquette of battle was observed. When one of them was speaking, the other never interrupted, but as a rule waited silently for his or her turn.

"Fine! Just fine! So that's how a daughter-in-law addresses her father-in-law, eh? A goddamned fine thing to say for a woman with two grown daughters-in-law and a grandson old enough to shave, isn't it?"

"And is that why a man with a great-grandson makes a habit of calling his daughter-in-law a 'frigid bitch' in front of her grandson? That's a fine thing, isn't it? The pot calling the kettle black!"

"What can you do with an ill-bred bitch? Lowest of the low! What could you expect from the daughter of a peasant? Nothing!"

"Listen to him! A filthy, slimy nobleman! I'd die before trading my origins for your scummy noble status! A noble, indeed! The real nobles must be all dead if the Yuns have become such high and mighty aristocrats! Who was it that was dragged about by the village officials, begging for mercy while his ass was flogged? Is that what you call a nobleman? The further you poke, the shittier the smell!"

However gifted in invective a man may be, he can never outdo a woman in natural talent. After being bombarded with this barrage of verbal shells, Master Yun had only two choices— immediate retreat or a shift to guerrilla tactics. In fact, Master Yun had a high opinion of his own sarcastic wit, but when in the course of this battle Ko exposed his bloodline to such venomous ridicule, he felt as though he were locked in a chokehold. The best response would have been the one his late wife used, which was to pounce on her, grab her by the hair, throw her down on the floor, and then beat her half to death with a mallet or some such implement. That would have produced quite satisfactory results.

Unfortunately, however, a father-in-law did not enjoy the same latitude as a mother-in-law in such matters. The established rules barred Master Yun from striking his daughter-in-law as his wife had. He couldn't help cursing whoever was responsible for that heartlessly discriminatory rule. Indeed, Master Yun silently prayed maledictions on the descendants of that legislator for three generations.

Pushed over the edge, Master Yun stepped into the hall and shouted,

"Hey! Kyŏngson!"

Back in his own room, the boy answered in a soft voice. Whether he had heard the response or not, Master Yun went on yelling. After a while, Kyŏngson came out warily, clad in short pants.

"Listen! Go this minute and fetch your grandfather! Right now, bring him back here!"

"All right."

"I hear people are getting divorced at the drop of a hat these days. He'll divorce her this very evening or I'll . . ."

There is an old saying that in the house of a widow a manservant with a large bell can wield power. Likewise, whenever Master Yun was cornered in a fight with his daughter-in-law, he invariably resorted to the divorce threat, dispatching someone to fetch his son. Yun Ch'angsik, however, when informed of the situation by the messenger, often flatly refused to come, or, if he showed up after being summoned repeatedly, he would say to his father,

"Very well, I'll take the proper steps tomorrow."

Unconditional though such a promise might seem, Ch'angsik completely forgot his undertaking the instant he left his father's house. Fortunately, Master Yun never pressed his son the next day, or any other day, to proceed with the divorce.

Master Yun repeated his thundering order to Kyŏngson, who was hesitating.

"What the hell are you waiting for? Go at once and get your grandfather, you hear?"

Only then did Kyŏngson walk toward the rear quarters of the house, feigning to change his clothes. It wasn't much of an errand, for all he intended to do was to go outside for a suitable time and return, or, depending on how the wind was blowing, he would just ignore the command and stay in his room. He could report later that his grandfather hadn't been in.

"You just wait and see!" Master Yun grumbled as he stepped down into the front yard. "Wait and see, I say! Up to now I've only been talking about it, but this time you'll see. He will have to divorce you or he'll no longer be a son of mine. Either way it'll be settled before the night is over. You just wait and see!"

Growling such threats, Master Yun stamped back to his own room. Ko promptly flung a rejoinder at his back, to the effect that he could do as pleased, that she wasn't frightened by the idea of a divorce, and that if he thought she would cry her eyes out, he was wrong!

Thus, this war, without beginning or end, was suspended by an armistice. No sooner had the two combatants retired from the battlefield than peace reigned once more throughout the house.

Everyone enjoyed the blessings of peace.

Samwol, one of the maids, was in the kitchen washing dishes with another servant woman. A manservant was tending the fires. The rest of the household, except for Ko, had gathered in the main room to eat supper.

There was the Seoul Mistress, the two sisters-in-law, and the head maid. None of them seemed at all concerned about the storm that had just passed; nor were they worrying over the fact that Master Yun's meal had been interrupted or that Ko had refused to eat. Not one of them had lost their appetite, and they had no reason not to be looking forward to the evening meal.

But then, as if to kill the aftertaste of the earlier fight, another quarrel, on a smaller scale, suddenly erupted. T'aesik had been completely absorbed in the row between Master Yun and Ko, but when it ended he returned to his meal. Just then Kyŏngson flew in, plopped down on the cushion where Master Yun had been sitting, and started shoveling food into his mouth with the old man's spoon.

To T'aesik the sight of this thieving, selfish rascal eating his daddy's rice with his daddy's own spoon was too much. And the prospect of all the tastiest side dishes being snatched away increased his foreboding. So T'aesik brandished his spoon, protesting,

"Hey! That's Dada's rice!"

Kyŏngson didn't even blink. Immediately he resorted to teasing.

"What are you talking about?" he asked. "Do you see his name on the bowl?"

"Eeeh! You're a thief!"

"Don't ask for trouble! Look at you! Are you going to hit me with your spoon? You want a taste of this? See this?"

Kyŏngson made a fist and threatened T'aesik across the table.

Kyŏngson's mother stepped into the room.

"Kyŏngson!"

"This imbecile's having a fit. He's calling me a thief. That's not my name, is it?"

"Well, what harm has he done? Be quiet and eat your dinner."

"Call me names one more time, you idiot, and I'll kill you!"

"Stop it, Kyŏngson, I mean it! If you don't quit, you know you'll get it from your great grandfather, don't you?"

"Bah! He doesn't scare me."

"Listen to yourself. If you don't behave, you'll be sent away! Exiled . . ."

"I'll have a great time, collecting insects, swimming, and mountain climbing; then I'll come back. So what's there to worry about?"

The Seoul Mistress walked into the room wiping her hands. She frowned at the sight of T'aesik still glued to the dinner table, not eating but pouting and sniffling his green snot.

"Sister!"

"What is it?"

T'aesik called to his sister in the hope of some indulgence, but when she just snapped at him, his only recourse was to start crying loud enough to bring his father running.

Sure enough, T'aesik's lips began to twitch, his face grew contorted, and he was ready to burst into wailing at any moment. To make T'aesik cry was to invite big trouble— not the sort of squall that had broken out in the earlier spat with Ko, but real thunder and lightning with force enough to demolish a whole section of the house. As a rule Master Yun was not tolerant of the mistakes of others, but anyone unlucky enough to make T'aesik cry was punished mercilessly for the crime.

"Now, now, eat your rice. It's not nice to pout at the dinner table."

The Seoul Mistress used a gentle tone in an attempt to soothe T'aesik. Kyŏngson's mother wiped the snot from his nose, at the same time sending an urgent signal to her son with a meaningful wink. Having decoded the message from his mother, Kyŏngson pretended to humor T'aesik.

"Grandpa! Help yourself! It's thanks to you, Grandpa, that your grandson gets a chance to eat this tasty food. Right, Grandpa? My grandpa is very kind. Right, Grandpa?"

Indeed, an inquiry into the family genealogy would reveal that fifteen-year-old Kyŏngson was the grandnephew of a boy the same age. T'aesik truly was Kyŏngson's blood granduncle, the half-brother of his grandfather. To dismiss this coincidence of age spanning three generations as a sign of the decadence of the clan would be easy. To call it a tragedy would be more fitting.

And Oxen Breed Iron . . .

Tadpole Sŏk sat all alone in the corner of Master Yun's room, cradling his tadpole belly in his arms. He worked for Master Yun as a kind of middleman, a broker, you might say in modern parlance.

Tadpole's belly always jutted out when money was due to enter his pockets. An unsightly thing it was, a belly filled with undiluted shit. He was a short man with no trace of a neck, a man born to wear the nickname "Tadpole."

"Had your dinner, sir?"

Tadpole sprang to his feet as he greeted Master Yun politely yet familiarly.

Master Yun had reason to be pleased at seeing Tadpole return this evening, but no glimmer of pleasure shone on his face. Instead, he muttered peevishly,

"And if I hadn't eaten yet, I suppose you were going to buy me a bowl of beef broth? Why do you bother to ask whether I've eaten?"

"Just say the word, sir, I'll be delighted to treat you," Tadpole countered.

However unprepossessing his appearance, Tadpole Sŏk had learned to read faces and to apply flattery when appropriate. Otherwise he wouldn't ever have made it as a broker entrusted with handling transac-

tions in the thousands or even tens of thousands of
wŏn.

That was surely it, Tadpole surmised, remembering
the loud shouting he had heard from the other room.
Something must have happened to irritate Master Yun,
so he'd come in without eating dinner and was venting
his anger on him.

Tadpole instantly sized up the situation and immediately tried to humor Master Yun with obsequious
gestures. No sooner had Master Yun loaded his foot-
long pipe with tobacco than Tadpole struck a match.

"Ah, sir, I wouldn't offer you a cheap bowl of beef
broth. At the very least, it'd be a full table loaded with a
good selection of delicacies . . ."

"Bah! They say a mother-in-law who lives too long
drowns in the dishwater in the end. I've lived long
enough to see plenty of surprises. Your offer is welcome— it's been a long while since a juicy slab of meat
slipped down my throat!"

The smoke from Master Yun's mouth wafted into a
dense screen. Tadpole smoothed his pants and stretched
out his legs, then he took out his own cigarettes.

"What a thing to say, sir! My offer to buy you a fancy
dinner is no big deal."

"Well, I can tell you, some people I know are always
talking about giving you something, but they never do.
Why don't you stop the chatter and order right now?
How about it? You can slight the old, but you shouldn't
slight the young, I know. All the same, blessed is the
young man who treats old folks nicely now and again,
don't you agree?"

A wide grin came to Master Yun's face. Judging from
this peaceful expression it seemed he had forgotten entirely his rampage of a short while before. But then,

this was only natural. If he savored his anger for hours at the close of every battle, how could he possibly survive those innumerable fights?

"But, sir, my invitation was not just empty words . . ."

Tadpole kept fidgeting in his seat, as if he would jump up and go out on the spot.

". . . I can go out this minute and have some food and wine delivered. It won't take a minute if I order by phone. So you really haven't eaten? Right, I'll order. . ."

"Ha, ha, ha! Seems a man'd have to knock you down on the floor to get a bow out of you. Enough empty talk. I know only too well you must have your reasons for such generosity."

"I beg your pardon, other motives? Me? Never!"

"It concerns the business we discussed this morning, eh? Am I right?"

"Not at all, sir. That was that and this is this. How could you take me for such a man? Heh, heh, heh."

"Whatever. But as I said this morning, it has to be twenty percent, otherwise no deal. Understand?"

Master Yun took the pipe out of his mouth in order to project a sober expression. Tadpole changed his position, leaning closer to the old man.

"It so happens I spoke with Kang on my way here . . . in fact, that's something I'd better talk out with you now, but . . ."

"You mean he said he'd do it, even at twenty percent?"

"Well, I was hoping you'd think this over a little more, for my sake, at least."

"What's there to think over? I'll lend him the money."

"Of course you will, but make it ten percent, please."

"Out of the question!"

"Well, I know that's what you said, sir, but let me

show you this seven-thousand-*wŏn* bill at ten percent per month and due in thirty days. Now, since you deduct the interest in advance, actually you'll only give him six thousand three hundred. After a month, he'll give you seven thousand, the six thousand three hundred plus seven hundred. That's not bad at all, is it? The man is in urgent need of the money, but from his standpoint wouldn't this be formidable enough? And here you are demanding twenty percent!"

"Indeed! Listen to me! The more urgently money is needed, the more utility it has, so much the more it's worth. So, he should pay more interest for the use of my capital, am I not right?"

"Even so, on your terms, the man will only get five thousand six hundred *wŏn* for a bill with a face value of seven thousand, and he'll have to pay one thousand four hundred in interest at the end of the month. Wouldn't he find it unfair?"

"If he finds it unfair, he doesn't have to use the money. I'm not following him around begging him to borrow my money or forcing it on him, am I? You're not making sense to me!"

Master Yun was making it into a take-it-or-leave-it offer, but even without Tadpole's argument he knew a seven-hundred-*wŏn* return in one month was nothing to sneer at. He was, in a way, compromising— twenty percent would be best and, depending on the circumstances, fifteen percent wouldn't be bad, and, if unavoidable, ten percent would do him no harm. . . . After all, the money was not invested, it was just sitting in the bank, getting musty.

"If, sir, you insist on twenty percent, he may refuse to borrow from you. . . ."

Tadpole, fully aware of Master Yun's frame of mind,

had at last captured the old man's attention. After waiting a while, he continued,

". . . so, without arguing further, sir, shall we make it fifteen percent? Even at fifteen percent, ten sevens is seventy, and five sevens is thirty-five, that's one thousand and fifty *wŏn!*"

"Why, my good man, you're supposed to be working for me as a broker. You make a living out of it. So how is it you always try to shift the losses onto me?"

"My dear sir! This will surely bring no loss to you! I just want to close the deal. They say stop a fight and clinch a bargain, don't they? And this is not just anybody's business, it's yours, sir, so . . ."

"Well, well, listen to you! Tell me, would you be pushing this if a commission weren't going into your pocket?"

"Huh, huh, well . . . ha, ha, ha. Now that you mention commissions, sir, the higher the interest rate the bigger my commission, you know. But you can't run the world on personal greed."

"What nonsense! If you live without greed in this world, you end up with your guts spilt for someone else!"

"There's some truth in what you say, sir. . . . Anyway, what do you think? How about fifteen percent, as I suggested? Yes?"

"Oh, I don't know! Do as you think is right!"

"Ha, ha, ha. You should have said so in the beginning. . . . In that case, I'll bring Kang himself tomorrow. When is a good time for you? You see, he needs the money before the bank closes."

"Well . . . Taebok has to be back. He said he'd return by tonight, so he should be here. When he comes, the money will be ready. So anytime tomorrow . . . but, this man is reliable, eh? You're certain of it, aren't you?"

"You can leave that to me! He owns a shop, you know, called Manch'ang Store, right next to Ch'ŏlmulgyo Bridge, sir. It's not like the man is a bum who wants the money for wine and women. He just needs to deposit the money in the bank by closing time tomorrow to keep a draft from being dishonored. The bank's sitting on all its money and won't lend to anybody, so everybody's screaming. You needn't worry about Kang. If you make inquiries about him, you'll know all there is . . ."

"What could I possibly know?"

Master Yun put down his pipe, rose to his feet, and took a bulky book out of the wall cabinet. It listed most of the small and medium-sized enterprises in Seoul, showing their business performance and credit worthiness— a sort of black list, a creation conceived by Taebok himself.

The credit worthiness described in this tome was not merely concerned with credit risks in the ordinary sense of the word— it revealed a man's total wealth as well as all his outstanding debts. Taebok updated the book daily, checking the newspapers and business reports and jotting down any new information pertaining to the changing credit worthiness of each enterprise. Thus, even though it was only a patched-together notebook of plain paper, a quick glance at the right page provided all the information necessary to determine whether a business was safe, as well as how much it would be safe to lend.

When a man from the countryside, especially a suspicious character, wanted to borrow some money, Master Yun made it a point to take a mortgage on realty as security, never lending without first having in hand a sealed deed. For those with businesses in Seoul, however, he would ordinarily make transactions on the basis of a note, if he knew the borrower well enough to feel secure.

Nothing in the world is more frightening for the debtor or more convenient for the creditor than a cognovit note. The moment a debt becomes overdue, whatever the circumstances, a distraint is executed, and the debtor's goods are seized for auction until the proceeds meet the face value of the note. Even if the loan is a swindle, the debtor has no choice but to pay if the loan took the form of a cognovit note. How could anyone not be afraid in such a predicament?

Through this convenient and foolproof method for peddling commercial paper, Master Yun floated twenty thousand to thirty thousand *wŏn* in loans each month, raking in at least three to four thousand *wŏn* in interest. In other words, his capital was breeding profits of ten to twenty percent monthly.

According to legend, the fall of Koryŏ* was presaged when all the iron in the nation was eaten by oxen. In modern times, however, everything has changed; all is turned upside down. Nowadays, oxen are supposed to breed iron. Of what could this be a portent? Anyway, money seems to be damned good at sticking with its own kind. Money makes money, doesn't it?

Master Yun removed his spectacles from the case hanging on his belt, propped them on the bridge of his nose, and began thumbing through the big book. Tadpole, more relaxed now that the business was nearly settled, smoked a cigarette as he waited for the decision.

Having located Kang so-and-so and his Manch'ang Store, Master Yun did a rough calculation, figuring that

---

*See glossary.

despite some indebtedness Kang was in good enough shape to warrant a loan of twenty or thirty thousand *wŏn*. So a piddling seven thousand, with little risk of any problems over the next month, posed no difficulty.

"Ah, well, he seems to be all right, but . . ."

Thus pronouncing a half-assent, Master Yun replaced the book, removed his spectacles, and sat back down. He picked up his pipe again and put it in his mouth. The earlier consent, though nothing was said, had been mutually understood to be conditional on the discovery of no problems in the credit check. This expression of consent was the real one, the effective authorization to proceed.

Master Yun had left a "but" hanging at the end of the sentence, however. So it was not a full but a half-assent. He meant to talk the matter over once more with Taebok when he came back. In the event Taebok thought the transaction unadvisable, Master Yun could still pull out of the deal very easily— he had made no commitment in writing; he had merely given an oral half-assent.

Tadpole tried to erase the terminal "but" and to confirm the deal.

"It's all settled, then? The money will be available for bank hours tomorrow, right?"

"Well, let's say that for now there's no problem."

"How can I commit Kang on that basis? You're the principal, so you ought to give a definite answer. Otherwise Kang can't feel secure."

"I understand that, but as you are well aware, I don't know anything about these matters. Taebok is the expert; I only act on his advice. Am I supposed to commit without sufficient information for a paltry thousand and fifty? Why, not even the whole thousand and fifty is mine, is it? After I set aside one hundred and five *wŏn* for your commission, I won't have even a thousand, and if something goes wrong, I stand to lose six thousand of my own good money!"

"Now, sir! If Kang were unreliable, I'd never have steered him to you, never. How can you say such things after knowing me for four, five years? Have you lost a single *chŏn* on a deal I recommended to you?"

"They say you should make inquiries even when traveling a road you know well. There are people, you know, who can snatch out your eyeballs without blinking themselves."

"Ha, ha, ha. Even at your age, you'll not make any mistakes! Making certain of everything is the way to avoid mistakes. Well, Taebok is coming back today, anyway, isn't he? You're sure about that?"

"It may be late, but he'll come."

"And if Taebok says it's all right, there'll be no problem transferring the cash tomorrow?"

"I suppose not."

"I'll bring Kang here in any case, around noon tomorrow. There now, that's a relief."

"You may be relieved, but I'm still rather reluctant— it seems to me I'm getting about a thousand won less than I could."

"Ha, ha, ha. Next time I'll bring you a really substantial transaction. Just be patient, sir, there're plenty of fish in the sea. With the banks tightening up on loans, everybody is desperate. People who've been buying land and housing with borrowed funds are really hurting; they'll be only too glad to pay, say, fifty *chŏn* a day!"

"In the present circumstances, who in their right mind would lend money for fifty *chŏn* a day? It should be at least one *wŏn*. It's not the lender who's desperate, is it? If the borrower is desperate enough, he'll pay that much."

Master Yun was totally unaware of the newly promulgated legal regulations for the control of usury. But even if he knew of them, such things were unlikely to frighten him. Ten years ago he was already charging interest in excess of the legally permitted rate. Besides, even if he got into a knotty predicament, he could always find a way out of it and be right back in business.

"Well, the deal is settled then."

With business concluded, Tadpole should have been up on his feet, but for the sake of future business relations, he decided to take full advantage of the opportunity to curry favor with Master Yun.

". . . and now, tell me, sir, have you really not eaten dinner yet?"

"I was interrupted in the middle of my meal. I was furious . . ."

His anger, forgotten until now, rushed back afresh and his stomach at once reminded him it was almost empty. The sound of his pipe as he knocked it on the ashtray seemed unnaturally sharp.

"Why, that's no way to treat yourself, no! Especially at your age!"

"It's just my wretched fate; that's what I tell myself!"

To Tadpole's surprise, rather than bursting into another fit of anger, Master Yun suddenly became calm. His face, which had shown no trace of worry a few moments before, abruptly darkened. His voice, not long before so vigorous, grew lifeless.

"I collect ten thousand bags of rice every harvest, plus tens of thousands of *won* in cash. A wealthy man like me, sitting on all these riches, goes without a meal! Can you believe that?"

Indeed, with the rice from a single harvest Master Yun could go on filling his stomach for a hundred, even a thousand years and still have plenty left. At the mere thought of the times he had gone hungry, the old man couldn't help lamenting his wretched fate.

"See, you, for instance, would be the first to call me a fortunate man, eh? Some good fortune I've had! You say it because you know nothing about me . . . a man in my situation is no different from a dog who barks all night long to keep thieves from robbing the granary. It's a dog's fate! A dog's fate, I tell you!"

Master Yun paused for a moment. He heaved a long sigh as he exhaled some smoke and stared blankly off into space.

Never in his wildest dreams had Tadpole expected to witness these grave looks and pathetic signs from a man whose face normally showed only irritation, complacency, or aggression. Being merely a philistine money broker, Tadpole wasn't cut out to plumb the depths of human emotions. All he could see before him was a man who possessed vast wealth, a group of heirs, and longevity. He was still in good enough health to hold his own with younger men. And yet, blessed with the best of providence, here he was moaning and groaning about hunger, his wretched dog-like fate, and so on and so forth. Pathetic! The old man had lived long enough and was drawing near to his end. With these thoughts in mind, Tadpole couldn't help looking up at the old man's face once more.

Three Old Coins and . . .

When Master Yun referred to himself as a dog, Tadpole was tempted to tease him with a request for a loud bark. However, such a jest would have been too impertinent. So, swallowing his true feelings, Tadpole consoled Master Yun with unctuous words, telling him that the head of a prosperous family with grown children and grandchildren cannot escape worrisome responsibilities of various sorts.

These consolations seemed to be passing in one of Master Yun's ears and out the other. Suddenly, his expression grew serious. He craned his neck and asked,

"By the way, have you ever watched people wash and shroud a corpse?"

There must have been some reason behind this question, but at the abrupt mention of wrapping a corpse, a chill ran up Tadpole's spine.

"You probably have. . . . What I'm saying is . . ."

Master Yun ignored Tadpole's hesitation.

". . . you know my old wife died last January, don't you?" he continued.

"Why, yes. Has it been that long already? Time really flies," Tadpole replied.

"Well, at the time, people asked me to come in for the washing and shrouding. So I went into the room where the corpse was laid out. I watched carefully— the ritual, I mean, I forget what they call it. After they put on the shroud but before they tied the seven knots, they took a spoonful of rice as if feeding a blind person, and they called out 'A thousand bags of rice!' Then, a second spoonful was fed and they called out 'Two thousand bags of rice!' That's what they did, I tell you.

"Next, they took one of those copper coins they used to use in the old days, a *sangp'yŏngt'ongbo,* tucked it into the shroud, and called out 'A thousand *nyang!'* Then they did it again with another coin, shouting 'Two thousand *nyang!'* And with yet another, 'Three thousand *nyang!'* That's the way they did it!"

"Yes, that's the way. People want the dead to have money for the journey to the other world, and they want them to be prosperous once they are there, isn't that it?"

"Yes. I know that, too. I saw it when my parents died. This wasn't my first time. I didn't mean to imply it was. What I'm saying is . . . I mean, my wife was no poor man's wife. I'm a wealthy man, right? She was a rich woman . . . but in the end, when she was dead and stiff, all she could take with her to the other world was three spoons of rice and three old coins. You see? When a rich man dies, he's given nothing for the trip but a lousy three spoons of rice and three coins, nothing more!"

Tadpole said nothing. He just lent his ears politely, feigning a grave expression. Master Yun quietly puffed on his pipe for a while before he sighed deeply and continued,

"Well, after giving the matter a great deal of thought, I've come to realize that once my eyes are shut, I, too, will have no choice. I'll be on my way to the other world with three spoons of rice and three coins, that and no more! And no escape from that, right? They are certainly not going to dig a giant grave for me. They won't throw thousands of bags of rice or tens of thousands in cash into my tomb, will they? And even if they did, what good would it do me? See what I mean?"

"Well, sir, that's just the way things are."

"You agree, don't you? My point, then, is that even I, with thousands of bags of rice at my disposal and tens of thousands of *wŏn* in my pockets— when I'm gone I'll be taking only three spoons of rice and three coins. . . . If that's how it'll be, why do I go on struggling for wealth, struggling so much that I lose the affection of others and earn the hatred of my own sons and grandsons? I never spend as I please; I never live as I please. Why? Do you understand now what I'm saying?"

"Yes, yes . . . I think I do. . . ."

"Besides, besides . . . do I have another hundred years to live? Even fifty? At most, I've ten more years before my legs stiffen. And once I'm dead, everything I have in this damned world will be robbed from me! Why, then, am I so tightfisted? Why do I quake so for a single coin? Every bitch and bastard I know detests me, and I'm without comfort or pleasure in my old age. . . . That's not all. I try desperately to scrape up every last coin, one coin more . . . what sort of pitiful destiny is this? What is this craziness all about? These are the thoughts that've been spinning in my head since I saw that ritual!"

For Master Yun to spill out his innermost thoughts so recklessly was so uncharacteristic one couldn't help but think he was actually undergoing a change of heart brought on by the imminence of death.

Host and guest were silent for a time. Tadpole studied Master Yun's mood, endeavoring to come up with some sort of consoling remark.

As far as Tadpole could see, the old man either was going senile fast or else was teetering on the brink of insanity. It was his hope that the old man would say something like, "Listen, young man, I no longer have any use for money . . . no use, so here, take this—it's my wish that you take it and live the rest of your life in comfort."

Tadpole could see no reason why the old man shouldn't disburse thirty or forty thousand *wŏn* on the spot, and his appetite, already whetted by poverty, was growing ravenous with blind greed. The urge to lick the boots of old Master Yun became more and more desperate.

"Sir?"

"Yes?"

Tadpole's voice was ingratiating; the reply he received was friendly.

"There's one thing I'd like very much to suggest."

"Suggest?"

"Yes, as a matter of fact . . ."

"Wait a second, you're going to tell me, just as you did the other day, that I ought to make a donation to the what-do-you-call-it, the school they're building. It's that again, isn't it? If so, don't waste your breath!"

Judging from this preemptive parry, Master Yun seemed to have awakened already from his daydream. He was back to his ordinary self—the mournful air in his voice and the pathetic expression on his face had completely disappeared; he was back to his usual lively self.

"Not at all, sir!"

Tadpole's heart fell as he saw his hopes crumbling before his eyes. Realizing that the situation now called for redoubled caution, he added hastily,

"Not at all, sir, you've already rejected that, so why would I bring it up again? What good could that do you, anyway? At the time I only recommended that gift for one reason— if you built a school you'd be held in veneration, praised by all the newspapers, and your statue would be erected. You'd be eulogized for generations, honored by posterity, you see? That was why I brought it up, just in passing . . . but then, on second thought, it can't be that great a thing to do. As you said, it'd just be a waste of money."

"Great or not, why would anyone in his right mind waste good money setting up something like a school? Why do things that benefit strangers? Tell me that! The greatest sons of bitches under the sky . . . you wait and see, I tell you, those philanthropist bastards will all be cursed! Soon they'll be out on the street begging for something to eat, just wait and see!"

In truth, Master Yun was neither senile, nor had he gone out of his mind. His thinking was clear and sober. Too bad for Tadpole, but such was the case.

Tadpole's endeavors to ingratiate himself with the old man ended up aggravating his ill-humor instead. Now Tadpole was in a sweat as he tried to mobilize his rhetorical skills in an enumeration of all the reasons why donations for public causes are invariably worthless. Only later, after completing this task, did he finally venture to return to the matter he had first broached before the conversation veered off on a tangent.

"Well, sir, it wasn't today or yesterday that I came into your service. It really breaks my heart to see you living in such distress, missing meals at your age. I myself have parents who are getting on in years, and I can't shut my eyes to your recent troubles just because you're not my own father. In my own way, you know, I always keep my eyes open to this and that. And this is not just idle talk, I assure you!"

"Is that why you offered to buy me a bowl of beef broth?"

"Sir! Listen to me, sir!"

"What is it?"

"I think you should . . . I mean . . . from the bottom of my heart I recommend that you take a new wife. Well, what do you think?"

Instead of answering, Master Yun grinned and flashed a sharp look across at Tadpole. The message of the look was clear: "Impertinent of you, but not a bad idea at all."

Tadpole grinned back, and moved one of his knees closer, tilting his neckless head toward the old man.

"Well, you're still in excellent health. What could be better for you than to find a thrifty woman, a middle-aged woman, set up a separate household somewhere nearby, and have her look after you? Now that your own daughter has moved in, I'm sure she can manage everything, but if you take a wife, for better or worse, you'll find her service much more to your liking. Besides, you're still a vigorous man, and whenever you get lonely in the evening or at night you can always get some consolation, hee, hee. . . ."

"I beg your pardon!" Master Yun exclaimed.

Nonetheless, Master Yun discerned a lot of sense in Tadpole's words. The last part, in particular, sounded so realistic that the old man, no longer content to grin and cast feigned disapproving glances, now was drooling as he removed his pipe from his mouth.

"Hee, hee . . . well, wouldn't it be nice, sir? Not another word, sir, just go ahead and start looking for a wife, sir."

"Well, seeing that you understand my situation. . . ."

At last Master Yun revealed his true feelings. Without further misgivings, he went on,

". . . and since you've raised the subject . . . well, it's not that I don't like the idea of having a woman around, even a crummy one with lice-infested hair, but at my age where am I to go, and whom could I ask to find a match for me? It's too unseemly, don't you think?"

"Ah, naturally you can't do that yourself, of course not! I know that, that's why . . ."

"Well, that's my predicament . . . I've no luck with my own relations, you see. Ch'angsik and Chongsu are the most ungrateful scoundrels on earth! I should have their balls cut off! I'll tell you why. You know, both of those bastards have two or three concubines, but they just turn their backs on me! If they were half-decent, they would have found me a woman, even a one-eyed woman . . . women are plentiful, aren't they? So, if they'd found a woman and given her to me, even a cross-eyed woman with a crooked nose, I could have her wait on me, like you said, or amuse me once in a while, right? But those bastards, they're too busy carousing and spending all the money I've saved. On themselves only, of course, never a thought for me! So you tell me, should those bastards have their balls cut off or what?"

This outburst reflected Master Yun's scheming nature and his ability to talk himself into feeling victimized. In truth, he'd been alone less than a year, actually only since the previous autumn. Until that time he had always had concubines lined up at his beck and call.

Back in the countryside, Master Yun had kept two concubines in separate households, and on top of that he had maintained steady contact with winehouse girls he found to his taste. And if ever he spotted a decent-looking peasant girl from the village, he had her retained as a house servant, on the pretext of massaging his legs. Such cases aside, in the ten years since moving to Seoul he had gone through at least ten concubines — *kisaeng* singers, fake schoolgirls, nominal virgins, and so on— concubines came in colorful varieties. All of them he discarded after living together for a year, or sometimes only for a few months.

Then, about three years ago, Master Yun discovered a suitable widow. He bought her a house right next to his own, and without much trouble got plenty of pleasure from her for almost two years. She was in her mid-thirties and tolerably good looking. Unlike most modern girls, she was not frivolous but quiet and understanding, and a good housekeeper to boot. In sum, she was a perfect find. Master Yun had a secret plan to provide for her, on the condition that she kept her health and remained devoted to him for the rest of his life. On his deathbed he intended to give her the house and a parcel of land that would earn her rents of a hundred bags of rice, lest she face a hard life when left behind all alone.

But then, something happened that Master Yun had been sure would never transpire— not with this woman. It must have been a trait she picked up while living as a concubine— they say bad habits can't be passed on even to a dog, but somehow she took to backdoor outings. In the end, she found herself glued to a boarder living in the neighborhood, a young insurance salesman, and one night she cleaned up all her belongings and all the valuables in the house and took off on a one-way walk with her lover.

Whether to cling to an old man and waste away the

prime of one's life, or to latch on to a virile young man, seizing the present and forgetting the approach of death—the choice between the two, the calculation of costs and benefits, is unique in every case. Still, Master Yun cursed her for a long, long time when he realized what had happened. In his eyes, she had cast away her own good luck, and he swore that she'd drop dead in some muddy ricefield. It wasn't so much that he felt any pity for her lot, but more because of the emptiness he felt around him. It was as though he had lost something, not a treasure, but something more like his favorite utensil. And so, out of sheer spite he vented his fury by cursing her.

At any rate, having tasted life with this earnest concubine, Master Yun had no stomach for just any *kisaeng* or fake schoolgirl. He wanted only the same sort of woman and the same sort of pleasure as before. Were it not for this acquired taste, he hardly would have passed the preceding months alone—he would have had two or three concubines by this time.

The one who had been sweating over the mission of finding the perfect concubine was a trinket peddler with a pockmarked face, a man Master Yun had been patronizing for years. When, after a long search, this peddler presented a candidate, Master Yun more often than not would find some fault to warrant a rejection and then harry the poor soul for not expediting the mission. On the other hand, Master Yun, an impatient man by nature, after a solid year of solitude was understandably fretful at the slow progress of matchmaking. Thus this cross and malicious old man inevitably cursed his son and grandson for their failure to drum up a concubine for him. Son and grandson lived as they pleased, picking and choosing woman after woman. So if they had a mind to, they easily could have located an exceptional woman to offer to Master Yun. But this filial duty meant nothing to them. They just refused to consider the wishes of the head of the family. No wonder Master Yun wanted to cut the balls off the bastards!

Whenever Master Yun summoned his son and grandson to the house to berate them about something or other, he always closed his lectures with the same reproach:

"You ungrateful, disrespectful scoundrels! You keep two, three women to yourselves day and night . . . and me, an old man . . . how can you abandon me like this and leave me to rot away? I should have your balls cut off!"

Master Yun was in the habit of making straightforward attacks. By comparison, his present snapping at them in the presence of Tadpole could be considered understated.

Meanwhile, having made good progress in his unctuous attempt to demonstrate his benevolence, Tadpole figured that if worst came to worst and the search proved fruitless, he could always retrieve a rotten piece of old lumber. But with things in the open now, he decided he might as well go all the way to whet the old man's appetite.

"Within the next few days I'll have something really fine for you, a wife, I mean. I brought up the subject for the first time this evening, but actually I've had it in mind for some time and I've been making inquiries here and there."

"The thought is greatly appreciated, but it's not necessary."

Such were Master Yun's words, but the glint in his

eyes, the grin on his lips, and his contented expression said otherwise. In reality he was thinking—Tadpole here is a man with a wide circle of acquaintances, a man with a talent for talking, in sum, a man who can be depended on to tackle this matter successfully.

"Not at all. Leave it to me. You just wait and see, sir."

"What if you fasten on to a *kisaeng* or a schoolgirl or the like? The kind whose only interest is to rob a man of his money, the impertinent and ill-mannered sort who go off day and night for between-meal snacks . . . the no good, useless kind . . . ?"

"Absolutely not! I wouldn't dream of bringing one of those to you. You'll soon see with your own eyes. Anyway, she'll be a widow, a mature woman, around fifty . . ."

"Damn you, sir! What use would I have for a fifty-year-old hag!"

"Ha, ha, ha . . . I know, I know, I only said that to gauge your reaction!"

"Huh! You're something else!"

"Hee, hee, hee . . . how about one in her mid-thirties, or just past forty, what do you say, sir?"

"Right you are, too young is no good, I know that . . ."

"All right, I see now. Just you leave everything to me, sir. Not too young, not bad looking, well behaved, and thrifty."

Just then the loud sound of a bell in the alley outside was heard. It was the newspaper delivery boy. The noise interrupted the conversation between the two men; tension suddenly reigned in the room. An extra edition was being circulated— major news had broken.

Since the local debacle and the Manchurian Incident*, the front had been moving gradually toward the

---

*See glossary.

south-central regions of China, expanding into a Sino-Japanese War. As the conflict spread, the newspapers were issuing extras more and more frequently.

When the bell announcing an extra heralds some natural disaster like an ordinary flood, the tension of surprise soon wears off if the bell ringing persists. People lose interest. But this bell meant news of the enormous disaster called "war." The growing frequency of extras heralded the spread of battle and the deepening of the situation, so with each peal of the bell people grew more tense, their nerves instantly on edge at the sound.

At the bell, host and guest fell silent. Imaginations triggered by the bell, each was envisioning the probable course of the war based on his respective knowledge of the circumstances of the ongoing strife.

"Another objective must have fallen somewhere, eh?"

Master Yun broke the silence as the echoes of the bell subsided at last.

"Well . . . must have . . ."

"I hear China is no match at all. Really, how can they dare to resist Japan, how can they try to fight the strongest power in the world?"

"Absolutely! The Chinese soldiers are terrible. When they hear the sound of gunfire ahead, they drop their guns and swords and run for their lives. That's why they have two kinds of soldiers in China, you know. Some are placed at the front to fight, and some in the rear with their guns trained on the ones in front to keep them from running . . . deserters are shot point-blank!"

"Sons o'bitches! Why the hell do they fight at all, when they have to put up with conditions like that? This time, too, they tell me, the fight broke out because they had their claws in Japan. Is that true?"

"It's true. They're such damn fools!"

"I say they'd be better off if they stuck to a quiet life selling pancakes, or peddling synthetic silk. It's absurd for them to be fighting!"

"I heard they picked a fight because, though power- less themselves, they have other powers to lean on."

"Lean on? Who?"

"On Russia, sir!"

"Russia?"

"That's right . . . and China wouldn't have acted as it did if Russia hadn't kept whispering in Chiang Kai- shek's ear: 'Listen, why don't you have a go at Japan? No? Damn imbecile, you, are you too scared to make a move? Go on, fight, go on! Once you start, I'll back you up, O.K.? Don't worry about anything, just go to it. Strike out, pick a fight, that's all you need to do. Good will come of it, you'll see.' That was how Russia egged on the Chinese!"

"I see! So it was Russia! But why did Russia do it? Wait a second . . . because they lost the Russo-Japanese War? Because of that old wound? And now, they want to settle an old score . . ."

"Not so, sir. Russia did it because she's got a mind to gobble up China!"

"A mind to gobble up China? Why, if that's what Russia wants, I don't see why she doesn't wrestle with China instead of . . ."

"You don't understand, sir . . . you see, the Russians are, what do they call it, socialists . . . yes, they're so- cialists!"

"Right, yes, I heard people saying those Russian bas- tards are like that . . . they took everything away from the rich and gave it to the farmers and the damned workers, isn't that right?"

"Right, sir!"

"Bah! What nonsense!"

"But Russia doesn't want to do it alone, so now she's trying to make China do the same thing!"

"China? Turn the Chinese into a gang of bandits, too? Into goddamn socialists? I don't care what you call them, but I know from experience that deep down inside those socialists are just plain bandits. Maybe you don't know it, but in old Chosŏn there was a group called the *Hwalbindang.** Same kind of thing as those damn, what're they called, anyway? . . . socialists, those damn socialists, and now . . ."

"I've heard of them, sir."

"Then, you know what I mean. The *Hwalbindang* was nothing special, just a pack of thieves, nothing more than bandits! Do you understand?"

"Yes, sir! Both the bandits and the socialists have the same idea— the poor ought to rob the rich!"

"Damn right! It's madness, all of it. Just because they're poor, they go stark raving mad. Out of sheer spite they turn into creatures like that . . . but, what were you saying? You heard that those Russian bastards are trying to turn the Chinese into a pack of bandits like themselves?"

"Yes . . . and it's not just China, they're trying to change the whole world!"

"What? Korea, too? But, wait a minute, I thought that in our country all those bastards, every last one of those damned socialists, was already arrested and imprisoned. Hasn't all that died down now?"

"But if China becomes like Russia, no good will come of it. It won't just affect Korea, it'll affect all of Asia!"

"You've got a point there! I mean, Korea is right next

---

*See glossary.

to China . . . surely it'll touch us! That won't do! Won't do at all. . . . Listen, others can take care of themselves, but what about me? What'll happen to me? It's big trouble . . . I don't know what to do. Even today, the thought of the run-ins I had with those gangs years ago makes me shudder. And now, must I go through that all over? Never! Over my dead body! How dare you, you bastards! Damn you to hell!"

A greatly agitated Master Yun shouted his lungs out, as if he had his enemies right before him.

"Well, what we should do is . . ."

"Tell me, who's stopping them from becoming rich? Tell me, who's ever stolen anything of theirs? Why do the bastards keep ranting and raving? I say each man lives according to the lot he's born with: some are rich, others poor; it's all fixed by heaven, the fate of birth. . . . Just because they are poor and others are rich, they're going to steal from total strangers to fill their own bellies? Does it make any sense to you? Answer me that! They should arrest all those bastards and cut their heads off! What'll I do if the world goes back to what it was in the old days? I really don't know."

"You needn't worry about that happening, sir."

"I don't have to?"

"Certainly not!"

"Well, that's reassuring, but . . ."

"The present attack on China is precisely to prevent that. You see, Chiang Kai-shek doesn't know he's digging his own grave. He's been hoodwinked by the trickery of Russia . . . he's heading for his own downfall. As you said, they'll all end up becoming the same gang. . . ."

"Right! Downfall and more! China will become just like Korea when the old gangs were on the rampage."

"In other words, duped by Russia's little game,

China's heading blindly on a rampage. If this madness is left to go on, it'll not only bring China down, it'll threaten all of Asia. This must be stopped, so Japan has stepped in to shake China back to her senses, slapping her across the face so she wakes up. That, you might say, is what this war is all about, sir!"

"Ha, ha, ha! Good! Very good! Now I understand what this fight is all about! It makes a lot of sense! A damn good thing to do, I'd say! The right thing, absolutely, to do . . . no doubt about it! And this time don't let those bastards off with a slap; they should be beaten half to death . . . beat the hell out of them so we'll never see that evil business again . . . beat them to a pulp, not a bad idea to break their legs. . . . Well, well, I must say this is splendid . . . there's no pillage and plunder in this war, you say, and it's not at all like an ordinary war?"

"Entirely different!"

"How admirable! Well, does anyone find life so depressing that such a change would seem welcome? Look around you. Plenty of government officials and policemen have been sent to our country to root out those gangs of fiends. Thanks to them all us ordinary folk can live in peace! And again, the war will protect us from those socialist devils, so what could be more admirable, more welcome than what Japan is doing for us! Indeed, it's most praiseworthy. We're really grateful for it! By the way, you're sure Japan'll win the fight, no doubt about it, huh?"

"No doubt, sir! Japan will be victorious! No doubt whatever!"

"I thought so, yes, I thought so. They say Japan is the richest and strongest nation in the whole world . . . that's a relief!"

Tadpole, who had been absorbed in the conversation, came back to his senses and pulled out his pocketwatch to check the time. Then he left in a hurry, saying he had other business to attend to. On his way out he didn't forget to reassure Master Yun that he would bear in mind the matter they had talked over and that in no time he would be returning to present a likely candidate.

Frugality for Its Own Sake

Once Tadpole was gone, Master Yun stretched out comfortably on his fancy mat, propping his head up on a wooden headrest. The sight of this pale old man sprawled all alone in the smoke-filled room, dimly lit by a thirteen-watt bulb, was somehow loathsome. At the same time, it called to mind a painting of some ancient ruin.

Lying there idly, Master Yun found life unbearably boring. If only Ch'unsim would show up early! She had agreed to pay a call after supper, so she would be coming for sure, but she was always so flighty and flirtatious, and not likely to come straight as an arrow. Knowing why she was late made him even more resentful.

Waiting for Taebok made Master Yun still more impatient. He was anxious to learn the outcome of the mission. Moreover, it was already eight o'clock and Taebok had to be back soon to tune in the radio for him. Since his dinner had been interrupted after only a few spoons of rice, his stomach was empty. Under the circumstances, if one of the women brought in a meal tray, imploring him to help himself, he would have condescended to yield to her wishes and have eaten with relish . . . the thought that not a soul in the house had the sense to do that irritated him all over again.

So hungry was Master Yun that he was tempted to

dispatch Samnam for a hot bowl of noodles. The mere thought made his mouth water, but he couldn't implement that plan for fear that such undignified conduct might come to the attention of the youngsters in the family.

Master Yun was curious who would show up first; it turned out to be Taebok. Taebok's appearance and deportment were rather pathetic for a man holding the position of a millionaire's manager, private secretary, and clerk. He wore khaki pants and a black jacket; a black tie was twisted around his shriveled collar; he wore plain sneakers on his feet and a four-year-old straw hat on his head. His face was sun-darkened with protruding cheekbones, hollow cheeks, and sunken eyes. He fit exactly the picture one had of a poor clerk from some township office in the country, a clerk just returning home exhausted and famished after a few days of traveling on official business. Not that Taebok had not in fact once been a clerk in a township office.

Taebok entered the room, but before he could utter a word of greeting, Master Yun was up in a flash.

"Is it done?" Master Yun asked.

Taebok had merely tagged along with a bailiff who had gone to execute a provisional attachment of the property of one of Master Yun's delinquent debtors. So the old man really didn't have to worry about the outcome; yet being a man of monumental impatience he wasn't about to wait for Taebok to begin his report.

"Yes, all went well."

As a result of long training, Taebok knew what attitude was best. He sat down quietly on his hunkers, and rather than offering his own account, waited in silence for his master's next query.

"What property was sequestered?"

"Actually there were about fifty sacks of rice in stor-
age, so . . ."

"Rice! What a stroke of luck! So you saw the notices
of attachment affixed, right?"

"Yes sir!"

"Well done! Now we'll buy the rice ourselves at the
auction for a good price! Since it's rice . . ."

"I've already taken the necessary steps to arrange in
advance . . ."

Taebok was not your ordinary servant; it was unthinkable that he would have conducted the business
carelessly. What Master Yun had in mind was killing
two birds with one stone: first, he had the debtor's
property under the provisional attachment, so the loan
was secure; and second, once the notice period was up
and the rice was auctioned off, he would buy it at a
cheap price through inside channels, thus enhancing
his profit beyond the original interest on the loan. The
taste of this double-dipping was so delectable that he
never let such opportunities pass by.

"Well, well, it all turned out very well indeed! So, you
treated those gentlemen to some wine or something?"

"I spent about ten *wŏn* on wine for them, but it looks
like we'll get it back and more, sir."

"That, too, was well done! With a bribe nothing is
impossible, you know. Now, go on in and have your
dinner. You must be hungry. By the way . . . no, never
mind, just go and eat. I'll talk to you later."

Master Yun was going to discuss with Taebok the
terms of the loan to Manch'ang Store, the matter he
had talked over earlier with Tadpole, but he decided it
could wait until later or until the next morning. Bearing
Taebok's fatigue and hunger in mind, he let it go for the
time being.

In instances not involving monetary loss, Master Yun had reason enough to look after Taebok's welfare. The man was a treasure, indeed. Rather, you might say, he was an extension of Master Yun himself.

His full name was Chon Taebok. Written in Chinese characters it meant "Great Perfect Happiness." To predict his ultimate destiny would be difficult, but up to this point in his life his happiness had been neither perfect nor great. On the contrary, his life had been quite devoid of happiness.

Master Yun and he were born in the same country town. Taebok had worked for five years in the local township office as a clerk, and for four of those five years he had been a bookkeeping clerk. His meticulous, diligent, steadfast, and yet quick-witted character had been what first attracted Master Yun to him. Later, when the Yun family moved to Seoul, Taebok came along with the household effects as an accountant, private secretary, and general errand runner.

For the past ten years Taebok's service had been faultless. Indeed, his performance had been so satisfactory in every respect that he seemed tailor-made for Master Yun's requirements. Shrewd, deliberate, prompt, and thorough in business matters . . . how could he go wrong?

If, for instance, the plan for the day included the purchase of three cakes of bean curd for the kitchen, at the moment of the transaction Taebok would feel strongly inclined to buy only two and a half cakes. However, since no establishment in the city of Seoul would market bean curd by the half-cake, he would further reduce the quantity and buy only two. In the end, his endeavor to save two and a half *chŏn* ended up saving Master Yun twice as much. What money-manager possibly could better that?

This is only one example of Taebok's commitment to thrift. Truly, here was a man devoted to master and to frugality! Were one to condemn him as a tightfisted miser, however, such a judgment would not be above the suspicion of having disregarded his human dignity.

That Taebok felt inclined to buy two and a half cakes of bean curd for his master's table instead of three, and that he felt compelled to buy only two because half-cakes weren't sold, was not motivated solely by a desire to save money. In other words, his conduct was not motivated entirely by a sense of the object— money. Whose money it was, or whose household it was, was of no importance. What mattered to Taebok was to spend the money in the most economical way. In that value of methodical efficiency, more than anything else, Taebok was zealously interested.

When he purchased two cakes of bean curd instead of three, or when he saved five *chŏn* by walking to the outskirts of Tongdaemun* on an errand for Master Yun, and only taking the streetcar back, though he had been given the fare for both ways, what joy Taebok felt the rest of the day! Again and again he would look with glee at the five *chŏn* he had spared. One might be curious about whether that five *chŏn* might not find its way quietly into Taebok's own pocket, but, of course, nothing of the kind ever happened. Never. Were Taebok called on to establish his qualifications, this pastime of his would stand him in commendably good stead.

Some people take pleasure in collecting rare old books. They collect the sort of books you wouldn't be-

---

*See glossary.

lieve anyone would possibly be interested in. Others take pleasure in growing plants. They put all sorts of tiny flowering plants in tiny pots, and in taking good care of them they even use a hair-tipped pencil brush to dust off the leaves. Such pastimes as these might strike others as softhearted, at best, and as utterly useless. To the persons concerned, however, nothing under the sun gives more joy and pleasure.

Likewise, in matters of spending money, Taebok's talent in limiting expenditures to what was absolutely necessary, a skill cultivated to the highest perfection in his mastery of the arts of saving, sacrificing, and haggling—this had become for him a true calling pursued for its own sake.

Between Master Yun and Taebok there was no such thing as "mine" or "yours," for everything belonged to the master and nothing to the servant. At the same time, Master Yun's trust in Taebok was so total that he had never fixed a monthly salary for him; the old man gave him complete discretion in providing himself with spending money. For Taebok to help himself to a million *wŏn* would not have been impossible. But his habitual monthly outlays were small and rigidly fixed: thirty packs of Tanp'ung cigarettes (in months with thirty-one days he saved butts to smoke on the last day of the month), twenty-five *chŏn* for a scalping at the barbershop, and seven *chŏn* for the public bathhouse. Such were his ordinary expenditures. Purchases of clothes, always of the lowest quality, and occasional transportation expenses (never more than ten *chŏn)* were to him extraordinary outlays.

Even under these stringent conditions, Taebok every so often performed a real feat of economizing, cutting back not only on the Yun family's living costs and the money budgeted for Master Yun's business endeavors, but also on his own personal expenditures, simple and utterly transparent as they were. The following example will be instructive.

Taebok took a bath once a month without fail(!) at a cost, as noted, of seven *chŏn*. Because he used no soap, no extra expense was involved beyond this seven *chŏn*, apart from a little wear and tear on the towel. After bathing religiously once a month, he decided, one day, to postpone his bath— he began to bathe once every thirty-five days. After six repetitions of this schedule, with five days saved each month, he had managed to take only six baths in the course of seven months, thereby saving seven *chŏn*, the cost of one bath. On the day this result was realized, Taebok was extremely pleased. Indeed, in his eyes this triumph was not un-worthy of veneration. It had been an exquisite feat, a sublime exercise of the divine calculative arts.

Back home, Taebok's still active parents were living without too much hardship as tenants farming Master Yun's land. His wife had served her parents-in-law until she died a few years back, leaving Taebok a widower.

Taebok felt sorry for his poor dead wife and con-cerned about his parents in the country. His lot as a widower he found wretched. At the same time, it seemed a potential blessing in disguise, though whether the blessing would be realized was yet to be seen. At any rate, being a widower allowed Taebok to entertain great expectations about the future opened up by his present predicament.

Taebok was an ownerless man, and there also hap-pened to be an ownerless woman, the Seoul Mistress, living in the same house. Accordingly, in principle, this coincidence of an ownerless hostess residing with an ownerless guest satisfied the conditions for a combination of the two. Of course, reality is a bastard and seldom displays any benevolence toward this principle of affinity, so no one could foretell whether Taebok's high hopes would come to anything in the future.

In the first place, both parties (or, rather the other party) had to have the same intention. And Master Yun had either to give his blessing to the matter, at least tacitly, or else drop dead. As it was, these factors remained unknown quantities or insurmountable obstacles.

If, let us say, the two of them fell head over heels in love and resolved to live together, despite the strong disapproval of Master Yun, then the land set aside for the Seoul Mistress's inheritance, land earning rents of five hundred bags of rice, would definitely not go with her. This would make the whole matter utterly meaningless from Taebok's standpoint, since the result would defeat the purpose.

Taebok, by nature, was no playboy capable of falling in or out of love with just any woman. Neither did he see any value in infatuation, so there was no reason he should find the Seoul Mistress, with her no-necked freckle pot of a flat-nosed bedbug face, tempting or desirable as a woman. The focus of his great expectation was to capitalize on his status as a widower, and this led him to perceive a certain attractiveness in this widow gilded with five hundred bags of rice.

At present, therefore, as a first step toward the ultimate goal, Taebok was hopefully seeking signs that the Seoul Mistress was interested in him. If so, that would portend the potential success of the whole scheme, a phenomenon to be greatly pleased about. However, even if the Seoul Mistress were to rush up and throw herself at him, declaring she couldn't live without him, without the approval of Master Yun her gilding would peel away, in which case Taebok would categorically reject her amorous advances.

By this time it was clear that on his deathbed Master Yun was planning to bequeath several thousand *wŏn* to Taebok. That was a sure source of funds, and he certainly had no intention of letting that bequest slip through his fingers as the result of a wrong move.

"Mr. Chon's back, so bring him his dinner, please," Samnam shouted as he stepped up onto the wooden floor of the hall outside the main room.

"So, Mr. Chon's returned?"

The Seoul Mistress, who had been talking to Kyŏngson and Taesik, replied in an excited voice and hurried straight out to the kitchen. Ordinarily, the Seoul Mistress couldn't care less who served Taebok's dinner. Even now she could have ordered one of her nephews' wives to wait on him. For her to show such eagerness, when she very seldom bothered even to look into the kitchen, was truly extraordinary.

Kyŏngson, who immediately sensed the uniqueness of this reaction, kept nodding his head and sticking out his tongue in the direction the Seoul Mistress had gone.

The Seoul Mistress, of course, was quite unaware of the impression she had given; in fact, her behavior had not yet struck her as in any way unusual. But then, whether she entertained any serious feelings for Taebok was yet to be discovered. The matter was, in fact, quite ambiguous, and to comment upon her feelings with anything approaching certainty would by no means be easy.

There is a saying: A short tongue can spit far. The Seoul Mistress thought of herself as the daughter of, well, of a noble family, and as the daughter-in-law of a noble family. Her father had an annual income of ten thousand bags of rice, and she stood to inherit a share of five hundred. Never once had she dreamed of comparing her status with that of the mere errand runner of the house, Taebok. And so, if things ever turned out to be such and such with words coming around this way and that, and if her destiny were to shift and be bound to that of Taebok, she might not strongly object, though it wouldn't be because of any great attraction to the man himself. The only plausible reason would have to be the simple fact that Taebok was not a female but a male.

If that was the reason, some might say, why on earth would she settle for Taebok, of all the eligible men around her, especially when she didn't even care for him? But the Seoul Mistress was not a virgin bride, and neither was she an experienced woman of the modern world. She was merely an old-fashioned widow, a woman of the old world. She knew there were people in the world, but she had no conscious awareness of the existence of males out there. This was not by any means because her virtue was as unbending and constant as bamboo and pine. It was just conditioning, a trained instinct like the instinct of a blinkered horse pulling a carriage to keep running on.

She didn't know why, but she simply and clearly knew that a widow is not supposed to have a second husband, period. Consequently, whether the Seoul Mistress would stick to her trained instinct when faced with a certain critical decision in the future remained an open question. Up to this time remarriage was still taboo as far as she was concerned. Not that she hadn't strained her pea brain on all facets of the matter. After a long, hard search for an excuse, she had come to the conclusion that it would be an offense beyond her powers. Granted, then, that this was how she felt, was it groundless to insinuate that her response to Taebok was exceptional? No. Once the die is cast, a reason can always be found.

Widows, not being genderless, are also at the mercy of the biological commander, and it is only natural for a widow to long for the opposite sex. The Seoul Mistress felt this longing, too. She was twenty-nine years old, and she had been alone for eleven years, ever since her husband died after one year of married life. As she approached thirty, the longing for the opposite sex grew stronger. For one not equipped with saint-like discipline, the facade of formal custom surrounding widowhood was scarcely strong enough to countermand the dictates of the hormones, expressions of an inexorable law of nature.

Thus, for the Seoul Mistress to long for a man was the most natural and the strongest of reflexes and, in spite of herself, she couldn't help but greet the opposite sex with delight. On the other hand, her whole world was confined within the walls of the house, and in that prison-like universe Taebok was the only specimen of the male of the species. In other words, at the simple mention of Taebok's name, the Seoul Mistress had an involuntary physical response, and her body was quicker than her mind at revealing her excitement, which with the passage of time became more obvious to the eyes of the others.

Still, this extraordinary response on the part of the Seoul Mistress's hormones had no ability on its own to generate any progress; it remained as yet only a material indication of future possibilities. Besides, no soundings were made to gauge her feelings; nor had any formal proposals yet been transmitted, so a toast to Taebok would be premature.

So much for that. However, if Samnam had had an ounce of brains, he would have taken the meal tray out himself and would have had sense enough to drop some nonchalant hints to Taebok by reporting how the Seoul Mistress had hastened to the kitchen and made a bustle of fixing his meal, picking out the best side dishes, warming up the rice stock, and so forth.

Had this been done Taebok would have been greatly encouraged and would have come up with some plan to deliver an affirmative signal in a more aggressive vein. But Samnam, a boy born blind even to his own feelings, was no man of leisure able to fathom the deeper designs of others. Ultimately, Taebok only found it curious that he had been served an unusually fancy meal.

Kyŏngson, on the other hand, was a clever boy. On observing such peculiar behavior from his grandaunt, he might have been expected to cook up some mischief. There was thus a possibility of something coming to pass, though nobody could vouch that it would.

An Anecdote of No Significance

When Taebok tuned the knob of the radio on the little table beside Master Yun's bed, traditional music poured out instantly, as if it had been waiting: "Tta-ang-tchi-tchi, chŭ-ŭng-chŭng-ji. Tta-ang-chŭng-ŭng-ta-ang . . ."

It was "Chanyŏng Mountain," a traditional Korean melody. The round melancholy tone of the bamboo flute and the dark nasal sound of the lute raveled and un-raveled, and in between was heard the delicate yet firm sound of a zither.

"Ta-ang-dang-dong, ta-ang-dong ta-ang-dong, chŭng-ji, ta-ang tang-dong-dang, ta-ang tta-ang."

As the first section swung toward its conclusion, Master Yun, who had been lying on his side with his pipe in his mouth, slapped his huge buttocks.

"Goo-od!" he bellowed.

Traditional music is generally considered to be a dig-nified art form, and in appreciating it one does not as a rule respond with such an outburst. But who would feel bound by such stupid rules of decorum, anyway? Master Yun had every right to cry "goo-od" when he found the music good. That such an ignorant man pos-sessed even this modicum of cultural sensibility in the realm of music might seem implausible, yet considering the time he spent rubbing shoulders with scholars during his tenure as a Master it should come as no great surprise.

Having finished tuning the radio, Taebok was about to withdraw to his own room when in walked Ch'unsim wearing a thin smile.

"Come right in. Why are you so late, you little bitch?"

Master Yun swore even though he was delighted to see her. Ch'unsim was not troubled in the least by his vulgar language.

"What would bring me early? I come if I feel like coming and don't if I don't. It's a free world!"

Spewing out this gibberish in one breath, she plopped down in front of Master Yun. He laughed blankly but kept his eyes right on her.

"Why, that beak of yours spins like the wheel of a gig! How come your beak rattles on like that?"

"What's a gig?"

"Be quiet, you bitch . . . I'm listening to some music. Why don't you get down there and rub my legs, huh?"

"No! Night and day that's all I do—rub your legs. I won't!"

Ch'unsim had reason to complain. She was young and so earned only half the full rate, but it wasn't right to ask a *kisaeng*, who paid her taxes, to rub his legs all the time.

Since the previous spring, Master Yun had been disappointed in love five times running; Ch'unsim was his sixth love. Since his loving concubine had run off the autumn before, Master Yun had endured the deep loneliness of a man on a solitary pilgrimage, not to mention the intolerable nightly boredom of a man without a companion.

The guest room was in good shape and ready for use, but there wasn't a single old man to pay a friendly visit to Master Yun. Out of desperation he might have gone out of his way to invite a *paduk** player, at the cost of wasting a few cigarettes, except that in his whole life Master Yun had never played *paduk, changgi,** or other board games. He had lived this long without ever learning to play dominoes, though most of his generation played. People attributed this aversion to games to the scorn and ridicule he endured as a child for being the son of the gambler Horseface Yun.

Without a companion to chat with, smoking his pipe all alone in an empty room with nothing to do except lie down and sit up in turn, Master Yun at times thought of killing himself to escape the boredom. Then, as luck would have it, in March of this year he had received a visit from a certain *kisaeng.* She had been hired on several occasions for drinking parties when Master Yun was down in the country for the harvest festival or for ceremonies at his ancestral tomb. She turned up unexpectedly at his house in Kyedong for the stated purposes of greeting an elder from her hometown and of informing him of her move from the country to Seoul. When she called she was accompanied by a pigtailed child *kisaeng* whom she introduced as her sister. Master Yun found this young girl most amiable.

"Little one, come and see me often. You can read me story books or rub my legs every now and then and I'll give you some money for roast chestnuts."

His tack was not very different from the ploys used by older boys to trick younger ones, when they say, "Give me that and I'll buy you a candy bar."

The child *kisaeng* wasn't likely to have sensed any underhanded meaning, yet she just kept on smiling

*See glossary.

without giving any answer. It was her sister, a full-fledged *kisaeng*, who told her to visit Master Yun and be his companion, arguing that children are good company for old people. She, too, probably didn't suspect any ulterior motives and was only eager to do him a favor in the hopes of opening up a channel of future business. As for Master Yun, it wouldn't have hurt for him to be called on by the big *kisaeng* now and then. She could recite some verses of *sijo*,* sing him a few folksongs, talk with him about this or that. . . . But that, of course, would be all. There was no reason why Master Yun should have any interest in the big *kisaeng*. If ever he had a mind to womanize, there was an over-supply of beautiful *kisaeng* in Seoul, and if it wasn't comely faces he was after, there was no scarcity of *kisaeng* with first-rate singing talents, so it made no sense for him to settle at the same price for this particular country *kisaeng* when she was plain both in looks and in singing.

On the other hand, from the *kisaeng*'s point of view, it made absolutely no sense for a *kisaeng* in her prime to neglect all her other business to make special calls on an insipid old man, to amuse him with inane games, and to wait on him without even getting a proper time charge for her services.

Under such circumstances, even if Master Yun's only intention had been to enjoy the companionship of a *kisaeng* as no more than a flower before his eyes, he still had to be the one to fetch her. If she came on command, and if her visits were repeated, then every third visit or so he would have to hand over at least a ten-*wŏn* note, to save face if for no other reason.

---

*See glossary.

But a ten-*wŏn* note— that one green piece of paper— was equal to ten one-*wŏn* notes, to a hundred ten-*chŏn* coins, to a thousand one-*chŏn* coins, to five thousand of the old *sangp'yŏngt'ongbo** coins— a fortune with which a wealthy man could journey to the netherworld thousands of times.

It was a sum of money Master Yun would never sneer at, and sneer he didn't. Moreover, in dealing not with a full-fledged but with a child *kisaeng,* he didn't have to bother with saving his face or with according her the proper treatment— all he had to do was hand over a few *wŏn* now and then. Whether she spent it on roast chestnuts for herself or on a bag of rice for her family was all the same to Master Yun.

Thus, the company of a child *kisaeng* was a pastime not only much less costly but also far more enjoyable. For Master Yun, a girl was cuter and more fun to have around. Besides, if it turned out to be more than a diversion, a child *kisaeng* would still cost less and be at once more informal and more entertaining.

It is in men's nature that the older they get the younger the women to whom they're attracted. The manifestations of this attraction vary from man to man, but Master Yun's way of showing his proclivity was most telling.

As the *kisaeng* sisters were about to depart after paying their respects, Master Yun, finding the occasion opportune, shamelessly begged a favor from the older *kisaeng.*

"Well, why don't you send her over to me once in a while. Now that I'm all alone like this, you see, I'm bored to tears. There's nobody to talk to. . . . So, if you please, every now and then . . ."

---

*See glossary.

The big *kisaeng* readily obliged with an affirmative answer before taking her leave. About three days later, Master Yun was lying alone in his room, bored to death and thinking how nice it would be if the little bitch would show up. *I bet she'll come, but you never know . . . the big kisaeng had assented readily enough, but why should she send the little one to me? Still, perhaps . . .* And then, late that same afternoon, lo and behold! Who should toddle in but the child *kisaeng* herself!

The exaltation was of the same order, probably, as the excitement felt by a young couple who, after great and anguished yearning, finally are able to meet. Master Yun was in heaven. Her arrival was an answered prayer, a wonder of wonders.

Master Yun treated his precious young guest gingerly. He had her sit down right beside him and had a wonderful time caressing her hair, staring at her rapidly moving lips as she jabbered away, or listening to her singing, which was more like the screech of some one stabbed with a poker. By and by the day turned dark, but when she rose to her feet to leave, Master Yun coaxed her to stay for supper. No sooner had they finished eating than he had the book *The Story of Ch'unhyang* brought in, and he got her to read aloud as he sprawled on the floor, watching her lips move. For a good while, indeed, he relished that golden spring evening.

Needless to say, more than once in the course of the evening Master Yun stopped her from leaving, but as ten o'clock rolled around, it was time for him to let her go. He went out of his way to call a rickshaw for her, and besides paying the fare in advance he slipped a one-*wŏn* note into her hand before she left. A truly Herculean effort it was. As he saw her off he told her to come again the following evening. And sure enough, the next day she appeared for an early dinner.

As on the evening before, Master Yun sat her down next to him and had her talk, read a storybook, and sing. Her singing resembled the screaming of a eunuch with a bad toothache. Commencing on that evening and continuing thereafter, he asked her to rub his legs. Samnam was sent out for ten-*chŏn* worth of toffee to feed her. Of course, Master Yun caressed her hair frequently throughout the evening, and he didn't send her home till it was very late. According her proper treatment would have required him to send her home by rickshaw once more, but he told her that since she'd be coming often in the future she couldn't expect to ride home by rickshaw every time. From that night on, he said, Samnam would see her home. Such, more or less, were Master Yun's words as he sent the girl off into the night, escorted by that bright young man.

Master Yun simply couldn't bear to part with a one-*wŏn* note, but with no rickshaw fare to pay, he was not unwilling to give her fifty *chŏn*. However, he deliberately refrained from paying her anything, for he feared that handing over money, even that trifling amount, would, if repeated, eventually become habit-forming. In the end, she would naturally expect to be paid on every single visit. Instead, he decided he would hand over one *wŏn* every third or fourth visit.

From that time on, the child *kisaeng* gave due regard to Master Yun's wishes and paid him a call every other day, or sometimes every day. Then one night, after she had been coming like that for some twenty days, something happened.

The night was still young. The pint-sized girl was mindlessly pommeling the old man's legs with her chestnut-like fists. Suddenly Master Yun asked her,

"How old are you?"

"Fourteen, sir."

There was still a twang of provincial dialect in her speech. "I see! So you're fourteen."

After a pause, Master Yun went on,

"That's enough now, come up here, won't you?"

He pointed upward with his chin. The girl sprang to her feet and moved over to sit down by Master Yun's chest. He pulled the pipe out of his mouth, put it aside, and began to caress her head.

"Hmmm . . . very grown-up for fourteen!"

The child said nothing.

"Tell you what. . . ."

"Yes?"

"Hmmm . . . well, you see, well. . . . Tell you what. . . "

"Yes?"

"Well . . ."

"Yes?"

Not quite understanding what he meant, the girl kept blinking her eyes. Master Yun, grinning broadly, wrapped his arms stealthily around her neck and pulled her close to him.

"Do what I say, won't you?"

"Good gracious!"

The girl bounced up in fright, as if burned, flung the door open, and took off running for her life.

It was a somewhat embarrassing scene, especially for a good-sized old man. But, then, well, nobody saw it. Even if somebody did, it wasn't the first time for a *yangban** to shit in a tattered hat. So there was no point counting it a disgrace to the family name.

---

*See glossary.

Master Yun muttered to himself that young girls are little bitches, that you can't treat them nicely, and that he should steer clear of them. For some time after, in fact, the old man passed his days and nights in oppressive boredom, just as he had done before. In time, however, the blunder struck him as merely a false step, just carelessness on his part. The shame he felt at the time was gradually forgotten, while the memories of the good times came streaming back afresh. Besides, that damned appetite, in driving him to snatch a taste, had ended up only exciting the worms in his belly; the hunger hadn't diminished in the least.

Master Yun's weakness for young girls stemmed from his old habits of manhandling the peasant girls back in his hometown; it was not a recently acquired taste. However, the girls back in the country had been seventeen or eighteen, sixteen at the youngest, and never once had he gone so low as a fourteen-year-old still smelling of milk.

Were one to draw a strict distinction in Master Yun's case, his appetite in the period of country life was for girls who were young yet mature in their womanly equipment. After he moved to the city, however, his palate altered and he was taken with girls of a different sort, little girls who hadn't yet attained womanhood. This change in appetite was not the same as the authentically biological drive revealed in his vexation at the trinket peddler's slowness in locating a concubine for him.

Master Yun's new appetite was so strong that he found it almost impossible to bear. At last, Taebok stepped forward. If one is fearless and determined, they say, a task is soon accomplished, and this particular task wasn't for just anybody; Taebok went out and made indirect inquiries through Mr. Kim, the proprietor of the barbershop.

By sheer luck, Mr. Kim happened to know of a child *kisaeng* living in his neighborhood in Angukdong; he was able to steer Taebok to her readily. Actually, the matter wasn't especially difficult; the city was awash with such small fry. When the person on the procuring side was a rich and dignified old man of seventy, residing in such and such a place and a member of such and such a family, a man seeking a little girl simply to keep him company, to sit by him and read or sing, and perhaps to rub his legs now and again, in such innocent circumstances no difficulties were to be expected. Even if that legendary paragon of chastity, Ch'unhyang, were reincarnated, she would have no qualms about sending her daughter to be Master Yun's companion. So much the less were qualms to be expected from mothers and fathers who were already inclined to march their little daughters out onto the streets simply to have one less unemployed mouth to feed. In fact, even if the black and ugly scheme were apparent, they would more likely than not have welcomed it.

Thanks to the introduction provided by Mr. Kim the barber, within three days Taebok managed to come up with a girl, barely fourteen, who fit the old man's strict stipulation that she should be under fifteen.

Actually her face was nothing special and she was as scrawny and awkward as a newborn kitten.

Master Yun, as expected, was quite undemanding as long as it was a little girl. He found no fault with her and greeted her warmly. He had her sing a few songs, stroked her hair, listened to her read stories, had her rub his legs, bought her some toffee, and in this fashion exerted himself to the utmost for the next several days.

Only when the girl was beginning to feel somewhat comfortable in his presence did Master Yun move on to the question, "How old are you? Hmm, very grown-up! You'll do something for me, won't you?" he said, putting his arm around her waist.

But this girl was cleverer than the old man, perhaps because she had grown up in Seoul.

"What's wrong with you, you old coot? Are you out of your mind!"

She stormed out in a fury, flailing the old man with abuse as she left.

Thus, Master Yun was disgraced for the second time. Though shamed, he showed no trace of a blush on his ruddy face. He was unable to ignore the situation, however. Crestfallen and agape, he just muttered,

"Huh, huh! What nonsense!"

Even after that, Master Yun was unbending in his quest. Four or five more prospects were brought in turn, but each time he tasted the same bitter draught, not of unrequited love, but of rebuff and disdain.

Master Yun found himself in a truly wretched position. Never in his life had he endured such disgrace— no less than five times between late spring and early fall his will had been thwarted by plain-looking child *kisaeng.*

This predicament was worse than any hardship he had endured in the course of amassing his great wealth. Master Yun could recall no other instance in his entire life in which he had failed five times running at an undertaking. Not that other means were lacking. All he had to do was send a message to the overseer of his country estate and he easily could have had a flock of fourteen-year-old girls, well, perhaps only a dozen or so, but surely enough to set up a small boarding school. As far as the tenants were concerned, their likes and dislikes had never been of any consequence. An order from the landlord had to be carried out without question, even if the order was to hand over a wizened old mother, . . . to say nothing of a little daughter. Regardless of whether it meant great joy or greater sorrow to the tenant family, they were to all appearances in no position to save their little daughter or sister from becoming a living sacrifice. It was as though she were a fat hen brought to the landlord at New Year's or for the Harvest Festival.

It was not, therefore, that the thought of taking a country girl didn't pass through Master Yun's mind, especially after the third of his vain attempts. Indeed, more than once he considered dispatching a letter to the overseer, asking him to send up a black-haired young chick. But this remained merely an idea, for there was something about it that led Master Yun to have second thoughts. If he had a girl sent up from the country, it would no longer be the kind of companionship he wanted from a child *kisaeng;* instead it would instantly mean keeping a concubine. And however you look at it, for a seventy-year-old man to keep a thirteen- or fourteen-year-old concubine would entail a serious loss of face.

Moreover, a country girl would be less satisfactory in other ways: she wouldn't be able to sing and would cost more since she'd often be wanting money for visits home and for who knows what else. Such were the inconveniences that led Master Yun to hesitate when he mulled over bringing a country girl up. But if this present effort with Ch'unsim proved to be yet another fiasco, he was not at all sure he wouldn't fall back on that option after all. From this standpoint, then, one

could say that Ch'unsim had a pivotal and subtly significant influence on Master Yun's future.

For over a fortnight Master Yun had been having
Ch'unsim tag along with him. She may or may not have
fathomed his unstated expectations, but by this time
she was no longer feeling so inhibited. Besides, of late
Master Yun had been paying more attention to her than
to other girls, in his own special way. And now, his mind
absorbed in calculations of various sorts, the old man
looked up at Ch'unsim from his comfortable sprawling
position. She was being difficult, shaking her head violently as she protested his request to rub his legs.

As Ch'unsim sat with her side turned toward Master
Yun the bobbed hair on the back of her head waved
rhythmically back and forth when she shook her head.
Once she took off her long hairpiece, she instantly
turned into a schoolgirl. She so liked the schoolgirl look
that she seldom went out in the hairpiece wearing her
long skirt, except when headed to the *kisaeng* guild or
when someone from the guild might happen to see her.
She always came to call on Master Yun in schoolgirl
attire, unless she happened to be coming directly from
the guild. To witness her sitting there singing a refrain
of an old folksong, such as "Ah, ah, it's the face of the
dead, ah!" was a sight to see, truly defying comparison,
but to her it was perfect. Master Yun might interrupt by
jeering, "Hey, little bitch! Since when do schoolgirls
sing songs like that?" but she wasn't the kind to let a
loudmouth ruin her mood.

Just then the radio program ended; the classical Korean melodies were replaced by the mad din of Western
music. Master Yun, his brow deeply furrowed, quickly
turned it off.

"So, you little bitch, you're not going to rub my legs?"

"That's right! I'm not a night masseuse!"

"I'll be damned! Well, if you won't rub my legs, sing me a song instead!"

"Singing's no problem. . . . After classical comes light. You need a pop song, right?"

"Aren't you the connoisseur? Not bad at all!"

"Well, they say a mule only scorns a meek master, don't they? I'll sing now, and you beat out the time, all right?"

"Beat what, silly! How can I without a drum?"

"Now, now! If you had a drum, I suppose you'd know how to play it, uh?"

"Ha, ha, you're a silly little devil, a silly little fox."

"Sure, I'm a fox, and you're a hippo? Ha, ha, ha."

"Come off it! You're silly, silly as Ch'orani!"

"Ch'orani? What's that?"

"There used to be a troupe of performers called Ch'orani—two old men, their names were Hong and Pak. They wore masks and jutted their heads about as they gibber-jabbered, cavorting about just like you. Old man Pak used to warble songs, terro, teroo . . ."

"Ha, ha, ha. Sing that once more, please. Priceless, it's too good to waste on me alone. Ha, ha, ha . . ."

"Ugh! There you go again!"

If someone had been eavesdropping without being able to see what was transpiring, he might well have thought two young children were at play inside. But if he had a peek?. . . Well, then, there would appear just what he'd heard described: a hippo and a fox amusing themselves playing games in their cage.

"Ch'unsim?"

"Yes?"

"You . . ."

"Yes?"

"Well, I was saying, eh . . ."

Crossing and uncrossing his legs, Master Yun dared not finish. He found it unbearable. The time was ripe for the old lines "How old are you? Hmmm. Quite grown-up. You'll do something for me, won't you?" In other words, the time had come for his confession of love, but repeatedly the words stuck in his throat. This diffidence was quite understandable, considering the fact that he'd already tasted the shame of rejection five times.

Between young people, it would have been "I love you!" Whatever the phrase, the ordeal of making the declaration is terrible, an ordeal shared from time immemorial by young and old alike, regardless of circumstances and without exception.

"That's enough now. Sing a song for me."

In the end Master Yun decided to let the moment pass and to bide his time a while longer.

"Right, all right. What shall I sing? At the Festival of Great Singers this afternoon you kept saying 'good!' during that ballad 'The Bird Song.' Shall I sing that?"

"Listen to her! There may be an old saying that a short tongue can spit far, but, my little bitch, if you can sing 'The Bird Song,' then I sure as hell can pluck a star from the sky."

"Listen to yourself, now! Why, I'll go to the guild office tomorrow and learn that song. And if I sing it for you, will you pluck me a star from the sky?"

"Who said anything about learning it? I meant if you sang it right here and now . . ."

"Bah! What difference does it make as long as I sing the song?"

"There you go again! I ask you to sing and instead you just jabber away!"

"Very well, hm, hmm . . . here we go. Hmm . . . As I went off o'er mountains and rivers, grace of our land from time memorial . . ."

The poetry of it was superb, but, mind you, the "memorial" in place of "immemorial" was hard to ignore. Unsurprisingly, the slides between highs and lows were off, and none of it was really in key. Ch'unsim was using the voice she always used in front of her singing teacher—a lung-bursting shriek like a wailing eunuch, creating the sort of music that would torture any listener except one sharing Master Yun's tastes.

Actually, the old man's exclamations of "Good!", though they did violence to the rhythm, were rather in harmony with her singing, and his compliment "Well done!" at the close of the performance conclusively proved that Ch'unsim was an extraordinarily gifted singer.

"Hey, aren't you hungry?" Master Yun asked, slowly rubbing his huge belly. Unsure what he had in mind, Ch'unsim replied in a bewildered tone,

"No. Why?"

"I was going to buy you a bowl of noodles if you were hungry."

"Goodness! Like a widow seeing a you-know-what for the first time since her husband died!"

"Mind your tongue, you little bitch!"

"It's just a saying, I didn't mean anything by it. If you're buying, I'll enjoy it to no end, even on a full stomach!"

"Very well. Let's order two bowls and we'll each have one!"

"Just noodles?"

"What, then?"

"Well, I'd . . . some sweet and sour pork . . ."

"What more can fit in that belly after a bowl of noodles?"

"Plenty more! Till there's nothing left to eat!"

"You're a regular highway robber! What does an order of something like sweet and sour pork cost?"

"About twenty-five *chŏn,* isn't it?"

Whether Master Yun saw it or not, the girl was well on her way to becoming a real fox; she knew very well that a dish of sweet and sour pork cost at least forty *chŏn.*

"Two bowls of noodles and one sweet and sour pork, right away, hurry . . . two noodles and one sweet and sour pork, right away, hurry . . ."

Samnam kept repeating these lines under his breath as he went out, like a Buddhist monk chanting a prayer to Amitabha. As a matter of fact, for Samnam to remember those words was very demanding, something more difficult than remembering not to miss a daily meal, a task that engaged his constant effort.

The room brightened for a moment, as if a shadow had just passed by. In that pacific interlude, a brilliant idea flashed across Master Yun's mind: Let's not be too hasty, he thought. Let's not blurt it all out at once as with the others. Best sound out her attitude in a more roundabout fashion, with stealth . . .

The policy was one of gradual but persistent advance. Her intentions had to be gauged carefully, lest things fall apart, lest there be a recurrence of disgrace, but if the situation began to look promising, then the closing in would come. This strategy seemed so eminently reasonable to Master Yun that a broad grin of self-approval came to his face.

"Ch'unsim?"

As he called her name while caressing her hair his voice had a quiet significance.

"Yes?"

"How old are you now?"

"Why are you asking that all of a sudden?"

"Well, no reason!"

"Fifteen. Since you last asked I haven't gobbled any more time, so my age should still be the same, shouldn't it?"

"Yes, that's right . . . quite grown-up, y'know . . ."

"I'm getting tall, but I'm still very skinny. By the way, how old are you?"

"Me? Well . . . I'm so old, I've forgotten my age!"

"Come on, no matter how long you live, you never forget your age! With beard and hair so white you must be pretty old!"

Ch'unsim gently stroked Master Yun's beard, which was as charming as a white horse's tail. Master Yun, with his free hand, began to pet Ch'unsim's other hand.

"Ch'unsim!"

"Yes?"

"You don't like me being old, do you?"

"What's there not to like? How old are you, anyway?"

"Truthfully? Do you really want to know?"

"I'm not dying to find out, but . . ."

"Shall I tell you?"

"Yes."

"Sixty . . . hmmm . . . five!"

"Good heavens!"

Ch'unsim's jaw dropped and Master Yun's mouth was also agape, and not without cause.

That Master Yun's actual age was seventy-two was a fact known to the whole world. For him now to deduct seven years and try to pass himself off as sixty-five to, well, to a lover, shouldn't necessarily be laughed off as petty and squalid. Indeed, an old man of seventy-two shortening his age by seven years and telling a fifteen-

year-old paramour he was sixty-five calls for a straight-
ening of the collar and some solemn thought.

It is not uncommon for *kisaeng* to deceive their customers about their age. Neither is it unusual for young
girls to misrepresent their age to their lovers. Once the
circumstances are known, a rational explanation is always forthcoming. But here we had a white-haired old
man of seventy-two who, in an attempt to sweet-talk a
fifteen-year-old child *kisaeng,* was fraudulently claiming to be a man of sixty-five. This, too, would have been
different—whether or not the girl saw through it—had
he slashed not seven but twenty years away and told
her he was fifty. But a miserable seven years! What
difference of any consequence could there possibly be
between an old man of sixty-five and one of seventy-
two? Still, in the hope of looking even that much younger to his fifteen-year-old love, Master Yun had
subtracted seven years.

What lever had been pressed in that stately and imposing body to produce such an unmanly utterance?
One is reminded of the old Confucian adage: "When a
man is idle, he fabricates unseemly schemes." Suppose
we modify the phrase slightly to suit Master Yun better,
and say, "When the tenants are busy, the landlord does
this and that"?

To be born a sexual being is man's inescapable biological destiny. Thus sexuality should by no means be
berated. In any case, it's not the sort of thing that will
go away just because somebody berates or scorns it. It
remains, on the other shore, beyond criticism or rebuke. Still, a virility of such barbarous dimensions,
recklessly ignoring the limits of age—seventy-two years
in Master Yun's case—cannot be written off merely as a
physical predisposition. It may be argued that Master

Yun was born with the constitution of Sindon, the Koryŏ dynasty monk renowned for his lechery, and that his constitution never would have reached its potential had he not been born with something extra.

Among the hundreds of Master Yun's tenants, a few at least must have been born with a constitution comparable to their master's. Yet is it not true that these men had had their virility sapped and their stamina dried up because they had to work like slaves in the fields to pay their rent in rice? Is it not also true that the lustiness with which nature endowed them had faded fast because not once in their lifetime had they taken a dose of restorative herbal medicine?

Moreover, even if one of Master Yun's tenants by some miracle happened to retain his sexual vigor into his seventies, his lot scarcely would allow him to lead a fast life. He would never dare even to fantasize about womanizing or keeping concubines.

Ultimately, then, it would be misleading in Master Yun's case to attribute his behavior to an inevitable biological urge. To speak of predestined dispositions was merely to make excuses; the real culprit was one's lot, what is called "environment" in modern lingo.

It's not that the ten thousand bags of rice brought to the man by his hardworking tenants generated not just a confluence but a perfect harmony of physiology, health, behavior, and temperament, thereby creating the fresh green Master Yun of today . . . though an interpretation along these lines has some value for purposes of argument.

Upon being told by the old man that he was sixty-five, Ch'unsim continued prattling on in her silly, teasing vein. She said things like, "Goodness, sixty-five, you don't say! That's really old! Wait a second, how much older than me does that make you? Hmm . . . sixty-five, less fifteen, fifty! Good heavens! You're fifty years older than me!" and so forth.

Master Yun made no effort to stop her. He only watched with a big grin on his face. Ch'unsim was merely comparing their ages for the fun of it, but the old man complacently took it as a favorable indication that her attitude was coming around. "She is willing," he told himself, only a little surprised at the large age discrepancy. Anyway, that she's willing is certainly a stroke of luck, so, let me think how . . . Such were the thoughts passing through his mind.

Love is blind, they say, and the saying is pitilessly true in the case of an old man like Master Yun. Blind through and through . . .

"You don't like me being old?"

Now, as a second step, Master Yun found it necessary to persuade her that being old wasn't nearly as bad as she imagined, or to convince her that although he was old he wasn't really old at all.

"What's there to dislike? An old man is better, no need to stand on ceremony . . ."

"Sure, sure . . . besides, though I'm sixty-five, I'm very strong . . . very!"

"Right. Even though you're old, you're awfully big, so you must be very strong, too, right?"

"If I had to, I could knock a tiger flat!"

"Ha, ha, ha. Why don't you go down to the zoo and wrestle with a tiger? By the way, if a hippo and a tiger had a fight, which do you think would win? Ha, ha, ha . . ."

"Huh! There you go again, talking silly rubbish!"

Master Yun peered up at Ch'unsim with a lecherous look on his face. He didn't know it but saliva was dribbling out of his mouth, and his body kept on twisting.

"Ch'unsim?"

"Yes?"

"Well . . . will you do something for me?"

"What is it?" she asked, but by the way she was smiling she seemed already to have sensed. Master Yun's confidence soared. Things are going well at last, he told himself.

"You'll do something for me, won't you?"

"Well, what is it?"

Master Yun grinned again, then furtively stretched out his arm and said,

"Come here, you little bitch!"

He pulled her firmly by the waist, quite relaxed as he did so, for his mind was at ease. Ah, but the little bitch all at once squirmed out of his grip.

"You're disgusting!" she shrieked.

Six times! If the truth be told, Master Yun was terribly disheartened. Six rejections were enough to make an impetuous youth hang himself several times.

Well, Master Yun had been feeling quite sure of himself because the bitch seemed to be responding favorably. Even in the throes of embarrassment he cast a sidelong glance her way, trying to figure out what the hell had gone wrong so suddenly. What he saw was yet another mystery to him.

The previous five girls had all turned tail and run, either weeping or cursing, but not this bitch. She had screamed and slithered away like an eel, but then she just sat down a little farther away. Far from crying or running away, she was smiling coyly as if to say "catch me if you can." The girl was killing him.

In any event, this being the situation, Master Yun still had a shred of hope . . . perhaps if he coaxed her gently.

"What's wrong with you! Ha, ha, you're something else! Why don't you stop being silly and come here? Now, come here, Ch'unsim!"

"No!"

"Why not?"

"You know very well why not!"

"You little bitch, so you won't do this for me?"

"I see now that you're a dirty-minded old man."

"Listen to you! Is this how you're going to be?"

"Yes, what of it?"

"Now, now, enough of that. Come a bit closer. I want to tell you something."

"I can hear you from here!"

"Ah, come a bit closer!"

"Phew, . . . so you can grab me again?"

"If you agree I'll buy you something nice, how's that?"

"Something nice? Like what?"

They say lepers used to hide in the rye fields, and when they glimpsed a child passing by, they would coax the child, saying, "Come here, little one, and I'll buy you some marbles" or "Come here, little one, and I'll buy you some sweets." One wonders whether this wasn't the same sort of thing.

Master Yun had not actually thought of buying her anything in particular— the offer just popped out as his coaxing grew more desperate. That was why he was at a loss to answer, despite her pressuring.

"I'll buy whatever you want!"

"You'll buy what I want?"

"Sure!"

"Really?"

"Of course!"

"You're lying!"

"No, I really mean it!"

"Then, will you buy me a ring?"

"Ree-ing? Come off it! Who's talking about such expensive stuff!"

"Hummph! What's so expensive about that? Downtown you can get one for seven *wŏn* fifty *chŏn* . . . a red ruby ring with an eighteen-carat gold band . . ."

"How much? Seven *wŏn* fifty *chŏn?*"

"Yes."

"Is that the truth?"

"You can go and see for yourself!"

"All right, I'll buy one for you . . . I'll buy it. So now, come over here!"

"Oh, no! You've got to buy it first!"

"Buy it first? Well, then I say no!"

"I say no, too!"

"Damn it, stop acting that way. You're like a little eel! Ch'unsim?"

"Yes?"

"Stop being difficult, will you? Just come here, and I'll take you to Ch'in Hill tomorrow or the day after to buy you the ring!"

"No thanks! Why not go now and buy it?"

"How can we go at this hour? It's night. We'll go tomorrow. Now, come here!"

"No!"

Master Yun actually seemed to have made up his mind to buy that ring. Not that seven *wŏn* fifty *chŏn* was a negligible sum, but he couldn't think only of the money. If sweetening up this girl, and a nominal *kisaeng* at that, only cost him seven *wŏn* fifty *chŏn*, he knew it wasn't a bad bargain. Were he to follow the conventional route, it would have cost him anywhere from a hundred to six-hundred *wŏn*.

To bilk the girl out of a ring was not Master Yun's

intention. He really meant to buy it for her either the next day or the following day. But Ch'unsim, whether from distrust or sheer mischief, wouldn't give an inch. She kept the old man dangling. In a way, Master Yun found her behavior hateful, so hateful he was almost tempted to give her a good slap on the cheek. If, however, he rashly tried to discipline her, she would get sore instantly and be gone the next minute never to show her face again. And that would mean that the semi-success he had achieved after five failed attempts would go down the drain. So, against his will, Master Yun resigned himself to a delay. All right, he thought, if I must I'll get the ring tomorrow as she wants and then . . .

"All right, tomorrow I'll take you to Ch'in Hill and buy you a ring, and from then on you'll do as I say, understand?"

"Certainly."

From the outset Ch'unsim had been cool and composed, showing not a trace of shyness. In fact, even when Master Yun lunged at her, she merely yelled and slithered out of his grip, with not the slightest tint of a blush beneath her earlobes.

"Promise?"

"Don't worry!"

"If you act silly like today, if you don't do as I ask, I'll take the ring, understand?"

"I'll give it back before you have to take it back!"

"We'll see. Come back tomorrow, then, after lunch. We'll go out together and I'll buy you the ring."

"I can come earlier than that."

At last the deal was closed. Just then, the clatter of the Chinese food delivery boy was heard in the front yard. Samnam entered and reported on his mission.

"Two bowls of noodles, one sweet and sour pork,

right away, hurry, as ordered!" he announced.

Ch'unsim rolled with laughter and Master Yun tut-tutted at the boy. They say a person in love is always hungry. And Master Yun had had his dinner interrupted to boot, so he ravenously filled his empty stomach with noodles and pork. Had he only known how well things would turn out, he would have ordered a nicely warmed bottle of Chinese liquor as well . . . that was his only regret.

Meantime, Ch'unsim was busily chattering and at the same time shoveling noodles and pork into her mouth so fast her cheeks were about to burst. She was already excited about the ring she would be wearing and showing off to her friends and to the people at the guild office.

After finishing his noodles, Master Yun let out a great belch. Then he started picking his teeth with the nail of his little finger, flicking the food from his teeth toward the window. He picked up his pipe and banged it on the floor.

"Mind you, Ch'unsim," he said, "don't you ever say a word about this at home! Understand?"

"Say a word about what?"

"After I buy the ring, I mean . . . after that, you know, you know what I mean, understand?"

"Yes, I understand . . . I won't!"

"Never!"

"I said I wouldn't!"

"I, for one, will be disgraced, and you'll get a beating. That wouldn't do, would it? So say nothing, you hear?"

"Don't worry. For a great old man you scare easily!"

"I can't trust that yapping beak of yours, that's why!" The truth was, Master Yun was beginning to have doubts about the aftermath. Good fortune tends to be followed by ill luck. If her parents found out, he would never get off with a seven *wŏn* fifty *chŏn* ring. A whole herd of her relatives would certainly come after him and pester him to death until they had extorted at least a hundred *wŏn* out of him.

Ch'unsim was so utterly absorbed in the prospect of getting the ring that she had pledged halfheartedly to follow Master Yun's command never to divulge the secret, but having sensed the hesitancy on Master Yun's part, it was she who acquired the upper hand. The old man had long since lost face, and he couldn't have cared less which of them acquired the upperhand, but he was greatly relieved to hear that promise from his love. From ancient times it has been said that to one in love, young or old, every word of the beloved is accepted as true.

A Surplus of People and
a Shortage of Goods

While our great-grandfather of seventy-two (purporting
to be sixty-five) was negotiating an amorous pact in the
bedroom with his fifteen-year-old paramour, elsewhere
in the house . . .

Out in the main room, Kyŏngson had finally finished
his supper, and his quarrel with his fifteen-year-old
granduncle was over for the time being. At present he
was lying idly on the warmer side of the floor.

The others in the family had withdrawn, and
Kyŏngson, much to his chagrin, had been stranded
alone with his disagreeable grandaunt, the Seoul Mistress, and T'aesik, the mere sight of whom disgusted
him. Worse, the Seoul Mistress, a storybook in her
hand, was busily moaning like someone with a bad
toothache, and T'aesik was grunting a steady stream of
nonsense as he stared at his Korean Reader.

It was a rare phenomenon, indeed, to witness small-
minded Kyŏngson sitting there in the room, for once
unannoyed by the noise of the other two. It was like
seeing a cat, a dog, and a monkey playing harmoni-
ously in the same cage. The truth was that Kyŏngson
was so engrossed in planning a certain scheme that he

was oblivious to his surroundings. The scheme he was racking his brain over was this: there was a rerun of *Morocco* showing at the cinema, and also a very good documentary on the Sino-Japanese War, and he was determined to see them both, but without any pocket money at hand, first, he had to pick the right target, and second, he had to figure out a promising blackmail strategy.

The fat old man? No! The warhorse in the room across the hall? No! He had taken to calling his grandmother "the warhorse" because of her habit of picking fights with anyone in sight. The Seoul Mistress? No! His aunt? No! Taebok? Well . . . No, not that stinking miser! Why he was so stingy with somebody else's money was a real mystery! Mother? Well . . . Of all the prospects, his mother and Taebok were still the likeliest, for Taebok was the Minister of Internal Affairs, and Mother, after all, was Mother. Here he was, future heir, twenty or thirty years down the road, to a hundred-thousand *wŏn,* but at present he had to rack his brain, that soft gray matter of his, to lay hands on a lousy twenty or thirty *chŏn.*

While Kyŏngson's head ached, the Seoul Mistress, her head propped up on a wooden pillow, was laboring with her seeming toothache.

"And then a singing beggar, strolling through the market . . ."

As her mirth grew excessive, a nasal quality seasoned her singing voice. It was music, all right. Just what kind of music it was hard to say, but music it surely was.

They say a person in agony longs to sing. Now it may not rise to the dignity of agony, but a restless mind is often enough to make one start humming. To sing of sorrow or to dance for joy is human nature, but when one sings out of restlessness, the trait in question is an animal instinct, a trait shared with the uncanny cries of a bird in search of a mate.

Humans, however, are also born with a second instinct, one that blindly takes over primary animal instincts, using them for other ends.

An adolescent boy, for instance, out walking a mountain path in search of firewood on a fine spring day, keeps time with his A-frame staff as he sings a song: "Yonder is Kalmi Peak, rain is on the way . . ."

Or, a *kisaeng*, not a bad singer, might lie alone in her room on a bleak, drizzling autumn day, lazily singing a song, rapping her fingers on the floor to keep time: "As we lose ourselves in ecstasy . . ."

Now, that young boy singing all alone deep in the mountains or that *kisaeng* singing to herself in her room, who on earth are they singing for?

It is what in Korean is called *hung*, you see, a sort of inner excitement. Like the bird crying to lure a mate, the youth's song was for the ears of some country maiden, and the *kisaeng*'s song was for her beloved somewhere. Instinct arouses both man and beast to sing, but a difference soon emerges.

A human sings as fancy beckons, without regard to others. Whether a country maiden is actually within earshot, or whether any man is around to hear is of no consequence to the singer. No such deliberate calculations ever enter the singer's mind. Restlessness of heart is all it takes to break into song, and once the feeling is out, the singer feels greatly relieved somehow, or more restless still, or more excited— many are the manifestations of *hung*.

The same applied to the Seoul Mistress and her story-

book, *Ch'uwŏlsaek*. Confucius, it is said, read and re-
read a certain volume so often its leather cover had to
be rebound three times. By this time the Seoul Mistress
had read *Ch'uwŏlsaek* more than a thousand times.
Still she had not let it slip from her grasp. No one could
have known for sure whether she intended to read it a
hundred thousand or even a million times more. She
already could recite the whole story from cover to cover
with her eyes closed.

This book, it is true, was no golden anthology of
poetry. Neither was it a Bible, or a Compendium of
Laws; nor was it the *Analects* of Confucius—heaven
only knows why she buried herself in it and would
never dream of parting with it. If the truth be told, the
only pleasure she derived from this book was the ease
with which the story flowed. After all, she had memo-
rized the whole thing by heart. Whenever she felt restless, she would at once pick up *Ch'uwŏlsaek* and lie
down. Once in a comfortable horizontal position, she
would clear her throat and commence the recitation.
Her voice rose and fell, and often her body and her legs
twisted and twitched in accord with shifts in pitch.
While absorbed in this poetic reverie, her heart grew
even more restless and she would tremble with ineffa-
ble joy, or feel refreshed and replenished—in other
words, *hung* came to dwell in her heart of hearts.

These recitations of hers thus were no different in
nature from the lively folksongs sung by a solitary
woodcutter in the mountains, or the melancholy chants
of a lonely *kisaeng* stranded in her room on a rainy
afternoon. Whatever the form of song, the more familiar
it is, the better it suits the singer. In the same way, a
Ch'uwŏlsaek known backward and forward was very
well suited to the Seoul Mistress's taste.

One might wonder, under the circumstances, if it wouldn't have been easier, more convenient, for the Seoul Mistress to lay the text aside and just lie down emptyhanded to recite the story. But a rickshawman without a rickshaw to pull would find running insipid, and a fan dancer needs a fan, even in January, or the performance will be absurd. Even though she knew the text by heart, the Seoul Mistress needed that finger-soiled, familiar *Ch'uwŏlsaek* cradled in her hands to get a full dose of *hung* out of her recitations. That is the truth of the matter, and that is why she was oblivious when the others jeered at her squeaky voice; that is why she paid no mind to those who looked down on her because she toted *Ch'uwŏlsaek* about day and night the whole year round; and that is why she started reciting early on this particular evening.

". . . and now, at last, with not a sign of his return . . ."

The *Ch'uwŏlsaek* operetta by the Seoul Mistress was nearing its climax when suddenly there came an extremely loud bass voice, defying any possible categorization, a voice crashing through the air with the force of abandonment.

"Rain . . . rain . . . is, fa-falling . . ."

"Sister?"

No answer.

"Sis! Ter!?"

"What is it?"

"I forgot!"

"Rain is falling, and the rice seedlings are growing."

"What?"

"You're hopeless! Rain is falling and the rice seedlings are growing. You still don't get it?"

"Hee, hee . . . rain . . . is faaalling, see-dle-lings gr-grow-owing, hee, hee, hee."

"Oh, that's enough!"

Finally realizing where he was, Kyŏngson leapt to his feet and ran out of the room and down the hall toward his mother's room in the back of the house. His mother was doing some needlework together with her sister-in-law. They were gossiping under their breath about something, but ceased at the sudden appearance of Kyŏngson.

"Why don't you stay put in your room and do your homework, and less of this running around?"

His mother's reproach was a reflex.

"When I feel like playing, why shouldn't I close the books and play to my heart's content?" Kyŏngson exclaimed loudly, walking right into the middle of the sewing things and plopping down. Half-stitched pieces of fabric were scattered everywhere.

"What's all this fuss? When it comes to studies you're always at the bottom of the class, yet you're the first to look for an excuse to play . . ."

"Now, Mother! Just because I'm no good at studying, will that make the family wealth go to somebody else? That idiot T'aesik spends a whole month on a single sentence, 'Rain is falling, and the rice seedlings are growing,' but he'll be a man with a thousand bags of rice . . . and do you doubt I'll be inheriting ten thousand?"

"You and your big mouth! Stop spouting nonsense, just study hard!"

"I'll study enough not to flunk. The students who get good grades are all nitwits. Well, except for my uncle. Isn't that right, Auntie?"

For some inexplicable reason, of all the men in the Yun clan, Kyŏngson had great respect only for his uncle, Chonghak. But his aunt's already protruding lips twisted into a pout and she jumped at the boy's remark.

"Don't even mention that man!" she cried. "Where on earth could you find such a fool?"

"My uncle a fool? As far as I can see, he's the best and the smartest in the family. Except me, ha, ha, ha. I'm so smart because I take after my uncle! Isn't that right, Mother? I am smart, aren't I?"

"Oh, shut up! All you ever do is jabber . . ."

"Ha, ha, ha . . ."

"He must be a dunce if he can't even get himself a concubine . . ."

Kyŏngson's aunt started grumbling, as if talking to herself, but then she paused and raised her head to thread a needle. The anger on her face suggested that a flood of vitriolic abuse against her husband, Chonghak, might burst forth at any moment.

"A man should never take a concubine, Auntie! He'll end up fathering a piece of squid like T'aesik, squishy-brained, isn't that right?"

"You don't understand! Nobody's stopping him from taking a hundred concubines, but now he wants to divorce the wife that lived with him through the hard times so he can remarry! If that's not a dunce of a man, tell me what is? And then, what next? Become a police chief? Bah! A police chief's ass-licker, that's all he'll be!"

"You really think Uncle wants to be a police chief? That's ridiculous!"

"That's why he's studying law, isn't it?"

"You're not even close. It's a grand mission for great-grandpa fatso! He wants his grandson to be a police chief so *he* can have something to crow about!"

"Listen, now, Kyŏngson, you'd better not go about blabbering that way, you hear me?"

Kyŏngson's mother admonished her son. If such talk ever reached Master Yun's ears, lightning would strike at high noon, and Kyŏngson would feel the thunderbolts. Chonghak's wife, however, was just getting warmed up, and her tirade became still more vehement.

"So much the better if he's changed his mind . . . not just any oaf can become a police chief. . . ."

"Why, just listen to you, Auntie! Were you expecting him to become a police chief, too? If so, you'd better get your divorce moving. The police chief is gone, never to return!"

"Watch your mouth!"

Kyŏngson's mother reprimanded him, casting a sidelong glare his way.

"But, Mother, what's so awful about a divorce, anyway? If I were a woman, I'd marry a hundred times and divorce a hundred times. By the way, Mother?"

"Shut up!"

"No, no, something different. Well . . . aren't you going to marry off the Seoul Mistress?"

"You're out of your mind."

"Come on, we've got to find her a husband. I can't stand the sight of her!"

"Are you looking for a whipping?"

"Oh, let him be! After all, he's right. As if my life here weren't bad enough, I'm on the verge of a breakdown with that nag of a Seoul Mistress on my back all the time . . . the day she leaves for good I'll start gaining back the weight I've lost!"

"Bravo! Good for you, Auntie! That's the truth! Let's marry her off, and you get a divorce and remarry. How about that, Auntie?"

"You little scoundrel, Kyŏngson!"

"What?"

"Cut that out, right this minute!"

"Ha, ha, ha! All right, I won't do it again . . . so how about letting me have fifty *chŏn?*"

"Damned rascal!"

His mother meant to be stern, but Kyŏngson's tongue wagging made her chuckle instead.

"Please? Just fifty *chŏn*, mother . . ."

"What do you want it for?"

"Is there a man who doesn't need money? Mr. Yun Kyŏngson, eldest great-grandson of the famous million- aire Master Yun Tusŏp, has no need for money?"

"I'm broke, so why don't you go ask your great-grand- father?"

"Sure, sure. He loves me so much he'll surely give me money. Come on, Mother, just fifty *chŏn*, please . . ."

"I don't have it."

Then his aunt intervened,

"Listen, Kyŏngson, why not ask the Seoul Mistress? Seeing how you're so concerned about her remarriage, she certainly won't grudge you a lousy fifty *chŏn*, will she? She might give you five *wŏn*, even fifty *wŏn!*"

She was only jeering, of course, venting her disdain for the Seoul Mistress. Kyŏngson, however, pricked up his ears and cocked his head first one way and then the other.

"The Seoul Mistress?" he muttered, eyes twinkling. "Help her to marry? Ha! That's it, that's it!"

Then he slapped his knee and quickly swaggered out of the room, still talking to himself,

"Yes, I've got it! I can't believe I didn't think of it sooner!"

Kyŏngson's mother cast a worried glance at her son's back. She was about to say something, but stopped herself.

The disturbance over, silence suddenly reigned in the room. The two sisters-in-law busied themselves with their sewing for a while, each sunk deep in her own thoughts.

"Tttaagrrr . . ."

At the sound of Kyŏngson's mother reeling thread onto a spool, Chonghak's wife came back to her senses, heaving a sigh deep enough to drown in.

"Well, Sister, I do envy you," Chonghak's wife said.

There was no reaction from Kyŏngson's mother.

"Your husband may live apart from you, but his heart hasn't frozen," Chonghak's wife went on, "and you have such a bright son . . . I wonder what atrocious thing I must have done in my former lives to deserve this wretched fate! It's like a living death! And when my parents married me off to this family, they must've imagined I'd be enjoying a happy, pleasant life as the granddaughter-in-law of a wealthy man!"

"You shouldn't talk like that!"

That was all Kyŏngson's mother could come up with to console her sister-in-law. Actually, she had run out of comforting things to say long before. It was the same lament, the same curse against fate, always heard when the two of them sat down together. It had lost its potency, and the same stale words of consolation, repeated day in and day out, had grown nearly as embarrassing as the complaint.

"What's so great about my own fate, I wonder? With a husband leading a life just as he pleases, it makes no difference if his heart is warm or icy. True, I do have a son, but he's already grown out of his mother's bosom, so you and I are sharing practically the same lot, don't you see? The two of us both are servants, slaves in disguise in a rich family. How could you . . ."

Kyŏngson's mother's voice, calm and restrained until then, suddenly became fretful, and her lovely eyes momentarily narrowed in displeasure. She went on,

"How could you tell this family is rich? Look at us, our clothes, our hands. Are these the clothes and hands of the daughters-in-law of a wealthy household?"

In fact, both women looked undernourished. Their hands were chapped and scarred, still not healed from the rough work of the previous winter, though the long months of summer now lay behind. Kyŏngson's mother was still dressed in the short rayon pants she'd worn all summer, and his aunt was clad in a coarse black skirt of cotton. Kyŏngson's mother glanced at herself and her companion and then she lifted her head and cast a look around the room. A chest made of fine red sandalwood, a dresser, a three-level cabinet, a wardrobe, some ornamental chests— the room was packed with sumptuous furniture.

"What good are all these things? What do you need all these for when you have no clothes to put in them? Better to have one suit of silk underwear than a hundred pieces of furniture like this! No good for anything except to look at. I've been longing for a bit of meat since summer began, but not once . . ."

Kyŏngson's mother had begun with the aim of consoling her sister-in-law, but somehow her own complaints burst out. At this stage the door to the room quietly slid open, and there was the sound of someone politely clearing her throat.

Okhwa had come. Okhwa was the new *kisaeng* concubine Master Yun's son, Ch'angsik, had been keeping since the spring. She hadn't been a *kisaeng* for very long, and had been attending some high school or other for two years. She had also been trained in India-ink drawing, and these so-called refinements were part of what Ch'angsik had found attractive. Her appearance, however, was far from refined. Her facial features were sharply sculpted, which gave her an air of coldness. Her eyes were quicker to laugh than her lips. She had a proud, even insolent look conveying an impression that she would be unfit for the role of an obedient wife, and the coquettish glint in the corners of her eyes bespoke her profession. Beyond this, her thick and sensuous lips insinuated something even more.

Okhwa had been frequenting the house of late, often enjoying favoritism from Master Yun. She expended some effort to stay on good terms both with the Seoul Mistress and with the two daughters-in-law. Undoubtedly she was well skilled in diplomacy, and though it may seem odd that she hadn't been a *kisaeng* for long, that was precisely how she latched onto a grand sucker like Yun Ch'angsik.

Okhwa always dressed in a schoolgirl outfit. In such attire, however, a *kisaeng* looks rather too polished; in spite of herself she reveals some of the ambience of her calling. No *kisaeng* would have the nerve to wipe that air out altogether, and Okhwa was no exception. Even so, given the opportunity, she would protest that becoming a *kisaeng* had been an unfortunate temporary setback in her life, and that now she had recovered her old self as a schoolgirl.

"You two are busy with your needlework, eh?"

With that significant smile in her eyes, Okhwa made a point of addressing them in a familiar level of speech.* When the two daughters-in-law rose to their feet to greet her, she responded to their bows by asking,

------

*See glossary under "familiar level of speech."

"How's everyone in the family?"

Okhwa put down the box of biscuits she had brought, and the three of them sat in a circle on the floor.

"You don't have to do this every time you visit . . . though we do enjoy them. . . ."

Kyŏngson's mother made a point of showing her gratitude. In fact, Okhwa never arrived emptyhanded.

"Glad to hear you enjoy them. By the way, any news from your husband?"

This remark, in a commiserating tone, was directed at Kyŏngson's aunt.

"The sun will rise in the west before I hear from him again!"

"Oh, my goodness! So little love between a man and his wife, what's to be done?"

"What do you mean, what's to be done? The worst he can do is eat me alive!"

"What an awful thing to say!"

Okhwa took one of the biscuits from the box, which Kyŏngson's mother had opened.

"Such a nice man," she continued, "I wonder why he is not more taken with women. . . . His brother and he, I must say, they couldn't be gentler! By the way, is he in?"

Kyŏngson's mother, puzzled by this abrupt question, asked,

"Is who in?"

"Kyŏngson's father . . . your husband . . . ?"

"Has he come?"

"Has he come? You mean, you haven't heard?"

"No, I haven't."

"Oh my!"

"Is he here?"

"Indeed he is! I ran into him a little while ago in front of Umi Hall. I asked him when he'd come up and he said he'd arrived on the morning train. That's what he told me!"

"He hasn't been home yet, though."

"Heavens! Seems a big problem is brewing here!"

"Nothing to speak of! Perhaps he has some urgent business to attend to and couldn't come straight here."

However she may have felt inside, Kyŏngson's mother's decent nature made her express her feelings in this way.

For a time the three women were silent. Kyŏngson's mother was thinking, "He must be somewhere in Seoul womanizing, but since he's here, he'll show his face at home at least once."

Okhwa, her own urgent business in mind, was saying to herself, "Now that I've established a pretext for my visit, I should move on to the main thing." And as for Kyŏngson's aunt, who had been busy inspecting the dazzling rings on Okhwa's fingers—platinum, gold, diamonds—as well as her costly dress of real silk, she was silently passing judgment on this woman, thinking, "What filth! A *kisaeng* concubine can never hide her true self!" A little deeper down, however, her heart was boiling with envy of Okhwa's lot, a leisurely fate allowing her to adorn herself with precious jewels and expensive finery. This envy engendered arrogance, and that haughty condescension in turn begot an insufferable conceit.

Meanwhile, Kyŏngson, having purposely put on a mask of discontent, entered the main room. The two singers were still racing neck and neck—the Seoul Mistress with her *Ch'uwŏlsaek* operetta, " . . . and now, at last, with not a sign of his return . . ." and the croaking bullfrog voice of T'aesik, "Rain . . . is faaalling, see-dle-lings . . . gr-gro-owing!"

Though he wore a disturbed scowl on his face, Kyŏngson exercised extreme caution as he sat down on the floor next to where the Seoul Mistress lay.

"What book is that?"

"It's called *Ch'uwŏlsaek.*"

The Seoul Mistress's forehead furrowed into a light frown. She seemed irritated at being bothered. But Kyŏngson went one step further and asked in a gentle voice,

"Very interesting it must be, eh?"

"It certainly is!"

"Well, I'll be sure to read it myself someday," Kyŏngson mumbled. After a pause he continued,

"I wonder if Mr. Chŏn finished his dinner. That meal table you set a while ago, it was for Mr. Chŏn, wasn't it?"

The Seoul Mistress felt her heart pricked, but she looked back at the boy with a calm and steady gaze.

"That's right. What of it?"

"Nothing. If he's finished eating, I was going to go ask him for some money."

Only then did the Seoul Mistress realize what a commotion she had made in setting the dinner table for Taebok. That was why Kyŏngson's remark had been so prickly. Yet she felt relief that Kyŏngson didn't seem to have sensed her intention. Even so, her mind remained restless and she stopped her operetta in order to gauge Kyŏngson's attitude more carefully. He, on the other hand, went on mumbling to himself.

"Damn it! That miser, that stinking miser! I wish he'd drop dead! He's gone too far this time, I mean it. That imbecile! Guess what, Auntie?"

"What?"

"That scoundrel Taebok . . ."

"Yes?"

"Wait and see! I'll kill him someday!"

"Why, what's wrong? Did he say something nasty to you?"

"Not exactly. It's worse than that."

"Well, what did he do to upset you so?"

"The imbecile's always talking to me about you! The bastard!"

In spite of herself, the Seoul Mistress felt her cheeks start to blaze.

"What does he say about me?"

"Well, all sort of things . . . 'Your grand aunt is such a gentle lady.' Once he said that, and he said . . ."

"Yes?"

"He said he felt sorry for you. . . . If only there was a child, if only you had a child you'd have some consolation, some rubbish like that he was saying, too, and . . ."

"How presumptuous! Who does he think he is to talk of me just as he pleases?"

Her irresolute voice didn't fit her expression of disapproval. She seemed more inclined to be peeved with Kyŏngson than to berate Taebok.

"That's just what I mean. Next time I catch him talking that nonsense I'll beat the hell out of him! Or I'll tell great-grandfather and have him kicked out of this house for good . . . the bastard! The miserable bastard!"

"Kyŏngson?"

The Seoul Mistress called his name in a gentle and dignified voice befitting a grandaunt, again picking up *Ch'uwŏlsaek,* lest the tension within her be revealed. The boy's reply was also extremely sweet in tone.

"Kyŏngson, don't be quarreling with others, do you understand?"

"I understand, Auntie."

"What Taebok said was all very presumptuous, of course, but you're still a young boy, and it wouldn't do for you to be quarreling with others! Even if you hear something unpleasant, you shouldn't pay any attention to it, you hear?"

"Yes, Auntie."

"Besides, don't go about telling people you've heard such nonsense. . . . Just let these things go in one ear and out the other, all right?"

"All right, I won't tell anyone!"

Kyŏngson rose from where he had been sitting. The Seoul Mistress was preparing to resume her operetta.

"Anyhow, I wonder if that scoundrel's finished eating," the boy muttered to himself as he opened the door to go out. Then he halted and, feigning hesitation, opened his mouth,

"Uhh . . . Grandaunt?"

"Yes?"

"Well, it's kind of late to ask Taebok, so . . ."

"What is it?"

"Tomorrow I can get money from Taebok to pay you back, so, well, could you let me have two *wŏn?*"

"What do you need that kind of money for?"

"There's something I need to buy."

Without further interrogation, the Seoul Mistress stood up, unlocked her wardrobe, took out two one-*wŏn* notes from the drawer, and handed the money to Kyŏngson.

That the Seoul Mistress had disbursed the princely sum of two *wŏn* was an unprecedented boon. Needless to say, never before had Kyŏngson approached her as respectfully as he did on this evening, nor had she ever before treated him so kindly.

"Tomorrow I'll get money from Taebok to pay you

back," Kyŏngson said as the cash was placed in his upturned palms.

"Do I look like someone who'd lend money to you?" the Seoul Mistress replied. "Don't talk such nonsense, just take it and enjoy yourself!"

So all things work out. Even if she had wanted to be repaid, she would have had second thoughts. A fox who has gobbled up a stolen chicken is not about to replace it.

Kyŏngson politely replied that he would do as told. He bade his grandaunt good night in a very humble manner, but once out in the hall he stuck out his tongue and wrinkled his nose in her general direction.

The wall clock in the hall struck as Kyŏngson put on his shoes. Already it was nine o'clock, so he only had time for one film, *Morocco*. He went out anyway, unsure whether he would go to the film or postpone the film till tomorrow and call one of his friends. They could have a lot of fun spending two *wŏn*.

The main gate was shut, so Kyŏngson went over toward the side gate. On the way he glimpsed Ch'unsim through the window of his great-grandfather's room. He stopped and thought a minute, then slipped quietly out the gate and returned a moment later.

"Samnam?" he called.

There was no answer, for Samnam had been fast asleep for at least fifteen minutes. Instead, Taebok poked his head out of his room.

In an irritated voice, Kyŏngson shouted,

"Is there someone inside by the name of Ch'unsim? A woman's at the gate asking for her to come out!"

Kyŏngson acted as though he were greatly annoyed by this bothersome errand, and then he walked out briskly through the side gate.

Before Taebok had a chance to deliver the message,

Ch'unsim had already heard and was rushing out of the room, barely pausing to stick her feet in her flat shoes. She flew out to the main gate.

Not only were Taebok and Master Yun taken in by this ploy of Kyŏngson's, Ch'unsim herself was completely fooled. She really thought someone in her family had come to fetch her.

Once outside, Ch'unsim peered up and down the lane, which was brightly illuminated by the light on the gate. She wondered where her mother was, for if someone had come, it had to be her mother. She was walking toward the mouth of the alley when she heard Kyŏngson clear his throat. Only then did she realize she had been tricked. She was about to become angry, but on second thought she ran after him, a smile beaming on her face. Kyŏngson, also grinning quietly, halted.

"Where's my mother?"

"At home, where else?"

"That's too much! I'm going back in to tell your great-grandfather!"

"What's this I hear? Phew! Must be a passionate affair going on, eh? Looks like there'll soon be a new addition to the household, a new great-grandma, no?"

"Oh, shut up! You're a . . ."

Ch'unsim made a great fuss of a protest, but not without a certain sense of guilt. She feared Kyŏngson might have overheard the whole proceedings in which she had contracted an affair on the condition of receiving a ring. Even if she was still wet behind the ears, she was already enough of a female to resort to putting on an act; crabs instinctively know how to pinch from birth.

"Well, why do you think I'm coming here all the time? Because I adore that ruin of an old man? You don't know anything about how I feel. . . ."

That Ch'unsim had been frequenting the house not out of any love for the old relic, but because the old man provided a pretext for her to see Kyŏngson— that was a story the truth of which she herself was not certain about. There was no point in testing the accuracy of it, since she had probably been coming to see Master Yun and Kyŏngson both. But at that particular time and place, she had to be adamant in categorically attributing her visits to Kyŏngson alone. This proved irrefutably that Ch'unsim was already a woman. There is not a female under heaven, it seems, excepting half-wits, who doesn't resort to cheating men.

It was on her third visit to Master Yun's house that Ch'unsim had first become acquainted with Kyŏngson. Around sunset, she had casually walked into the old man's room, expecting to see him, but instead had found a little master with a shaved head twirling the knobs of the radio on the table. She had been slightly embarrassed, but upon noticing that he wasn't bad-looking at all, she thought it would be fun to talk with him.

As for Kyŏngson, he was very startled at first, thinking he had been caught red handed by the fat old man. But once he realized it was some girl standing there, he kept staring her straight in the face. She's not one of the girls who used to frequent this room, he told himself. They were all ugly as sin . . . this one is not bad at all . . . it'll be fun to see what she's like.

First impressions are known to be of the utmost importance in an affair. They made a perfect first impression on each other. They stared at each other for a long while, the one standing there with her hands on the sliding door, and the other sitting with his fingers glued to the radio knobs. At last, Kyŏngson broke the silence.

"Who are you?" he asked.

Notwithstanding the pleasant surprise and curiosity revealed in his eyes, he seemed overly conscious of being on home terrain as he got to his feet and questioned her in the tone of an interrogator.

Ch'unsim's reply was no less firm.

"Who are you?" she asked.

As one coming to call at the behest of the head of the family, she knew she had nothing to fear from this youngster, little master or not. Finding this impudent girl quite ill-mannered, Kyŏngson moved right up to her nose and glared at her.

"Well, I'm the young master of this family."

"Bah! If you were the old master instead of the young one, you would've eaten me alive."

"Little girl, aren't you daring!"

"What if I am? You're like a little chick strutting around the nest, lording it over a newcomer just because you're at home!"

"Watch your mouth! You want a taste of this fist?"

"Go right ahead, big talker!"

"You mean it?"

"Sure!"

"All right!

Kyŏngson raised his fist under Ch'unsim's nose, but she didn't even blink; she just kept smiling. Grins come in all kinds, but Ch'unsim's smile exuded friendliness.

"Why don't you hit me?"

"I don't want to make you cry!"

"Me? Cry?"

"What's your name?"

"You already know it!"

"I know your name?"

"Sure you do!"

"Me?"

"You've been calling me 'you', 'you', haven't you?"

"I see! Ha, ha, ha . . . well, what might be the name of this honorable maiden?"

"Who said I was a maiden? Hee, hee, hee . . ."

"Ha, ha, ha . . . what is it? Your name?"

"Ch'unsim."

"Umm . . . Ch'unsim . . . and how old are you?"

"Fifteen."

"Ha! So am I!"

"Really?"

"Yep!"

"Your name?"

"Kyŏngson."

"Kyŏngson? Like the movie actor?"

"No! How dare you compare me to such a character!"

"Phew!"

"You better not!"

"What if I do?"

"You really want a punch in the nose?"

Kyŏngson raised his fist again. This time the air was much less tense than before, and she knew he had no intention of striking her. Still, she made a big fuss, plunging into a song and dance that ended in an offer of unconditional surrender.

"Then, you swear you'll never say such things again?"

"I swear!"

"Well, and . . ."

"And what?"

"Nothing . . . by the way, are you a *kisaeng* like the others?"

"Yes."

"I see. Then . . . ?"

"Then, what?"

"Then, you are carried around on rickshaws and serve at *kisaeng* restaurants?"

"Yes!"

"And then?"

"And then what?"

"You ride in a rickshaw to a *kisaeng* restaurant and then . . . ?"

"I sing to the customers, and serve them drinks . . ."

"And then what?"

"When it's over, I ride home in a rickshaw . . ."

"That's all?"

"That's all!"

"What about money? Don't you get any money?"

"Why shouldn't I?"

"How much?"

"One *wŏn* fifty *chŏn* an hour . . ."

"Not bad! For how many hours?"

"It depends . . ."

"Do you dress this way when you go there?"

"That'd be asking for big trouble! I have to wear my hair up and dress in a long-skirted *hanbok*, and . . ."

They had heard Master Yun cough as he came in the main gate, so the conversation had stopped then and there. However, Kyŏngson had managed to say hurriedly,

"Come on over to my room there, in the back of the house, we can talk more, O.K.?"

From that day on, the mutual fascination between the two youngsters developed at an alarming pace. The stage for their encounters was usually Kyŏngson's room, or a movie theater, or a certain Chinese restaurant with an ornate back door in Angukdong.

Before long Kyŏngson presented Ch'unsim with sumptuous gifts, like Coty powder and perfumes, and she, though not very talented at needlework, gave him a soft handkerchief on which she had embroidered both their names. Such, more or less, had been the course of their relationship. And now back to the scene in the alley that night.

Ch'unsim had made such a fuss at having been wronged that Kyŏngson was inclined to believe her (despite the fact that he had never suspected her), and he regretted that this practical joke had gone too far. Of all the male creatures walking the earth, perhaps there is not one immune to the devices of the female of the species.

"Let's go to a movie."

With this abrupt remark Kyŏngson broke a long silence. This tactless maneuver caused Ch'unsim instantly to brighten, her feigned anger forgotten. The effect would have been the same, even if her bad humor had been authentic.

"It's late, you know."

"It's all right."

"The old man . . ."

"You can make up some excuse, can't you?"

Ch'unsim was all smiles as she went back to the house. She stepped up on the porch and said,

"Sir! I've got to go home now!"

Master Yun poked his head out of his room, his white beard hanging down over the translucent paper of the door.

"Very well! Someone come to fetch you?"

"Yes . . . my father's taken ill, so my mother came to get me!"

"Hurry home, then. What did she say he's got?"

"She doesn't know. Suddenly, he just . . ."

"Sounds like he's gotten some bad food, an intestinal

disorder . . . can lead to convulsions . . ."

"Well, I'm not sure what it is."

"Hurry on, then. If it is an intestinal problem, come back for some medicine, I have some good Chinese pills."

"I will."

"Now, go ahead, quickly . . . and, you're coming again tomorrow, aren't you? To go buy the ring . . ."

"Yes, I'm coming."

"Without fail?"

"Yes, without fail."

"I'll be waiting for you . . . I'll buy the ring for you, all right?"

"All right. Good night, then."

"Good night . . . can you go alone?"

"Oh, don't worry! I'll be fine."

"If you're scared, Samnam'll go with you."

"What's there to be scared about?"

"Very well, run along now and be sure to come around noon tomorrow. Then, we'll go to Ch'in Hill for the ring, understand?"

"Yes."

"Good-bye, then!"

"Good-bye!"

"Good, off with you, hurry home . . . we'll go buy the ring tomorrow, won't we?"

The word "ring" seemed to fly out every time he opened his mouth. He had cause to be concerned, no doubt. With her father ill, she might be prevented from coming the next day— that would mean the affair would have to be postponed yet again. That was why Master Yun had volunteered to supply those expensive Chinese pills for her father.

In all events, here was a girl shared between an old

man and his great-grandson, notwithstanding the age difference. It was, one might say, a very economical arrangement to deal with a shortage of women among the men of the family.

The merits and demerits of economizing aside, the fact that an oversupply of women within the family was coupled with a shortage of females without, viewed from a modern standpoint, was a lamentable predicament in which, due to a lack of regulation, there had arisen the contradiction of overproduction and scarcity, a crisis of supply and demand.

A Brief History of the
Universal Trade

That same night around five minutes past nine, in other words, about the same time that Okhwa, Ch'angsik's second concubine who had dropped by the house, was telling her two prospective daughters-in-law, Kyŏngson's mother and aunt, how earlier that day in front of Umi Hall she had run into Chongsu, the same Chongsu who had not showed his face at the Yun house; Chongsu, accompanied by his gangly lackey Pyongho, was visiting a pimp in the Tonggwan red-light district.

Chongsu needs no further introduction: he was, of course, the eldest grandson of Master Yun, first son of Ch'angsik, and father of Kyŏngson. He had moved back to the family's home estate in the country where he worked as a township official in a calculated step toward the ultimate goal of obtaining a county magistracy, to the greater glory of the Yun clan. He also was the elder brother of Chonghak, who was studying law at some university in Tokyo with the objective one day of becoming a police chief. Now that all these circumstances have been concatenated, Chongsu's status and prospects assumed very considerable proportions.

In old China there was a man called the Duke of Zhou. He was the son of King Wen, the younger brother of King Wu, and also an uncle of the monarch in his own time. His high birth, splendid lot, and close connections with the powerful made him renowned for his capacity to keep the whole nation under his thumb. Yet the Duke of Zhou had nothing on Chongsu, who was in no measure inferior to that famous noble.

One might wonder how Chongsu, a man of such elevated rank, had come to walk the streets of this seedy district, of all the places one might go in search of a sympathetic woman. Underneath appearances, of course, there are always little twists and turns in the hows and whys.

Chongsu was twenty-nine years old. He was handsome like most of the Yun men, but it was a kind of handsomeness that gave the impression of weakness of character, of mild indecisiveness at best. Were a physiognomist to examine his face, he might read wealth on his fine, broad forehead. But then, one never can tell. These days even the physiognomists may be senile, and in the modern age it's the god-awful ugly mugs that seem to attract all the money.

Chongsu was seventeen when he first came to Seoul to take the high school entrance examination; he had failed forthwith. He stayed on in Seoul, enrolled at some cramming institute, and pretended to prepare for another attempt the following year, only to fail again. At nineteen he failed for the third time and a year later, at the age of twenty, he lacked the nerve to take the exam with students years younger than he. Moreover, his eligibility had lapsed.

That same year, it was the Year of the Snake, Chongsu's younger brother, Chonghak, not only passed the high school entrance exam, but he got the highest score and was offered admittance to a top school. It was as though in one step Chonghak had made up for the three consecutive failures of his brother.

By then about half the family had moved to Seoul, but Chongsu was in such a sorry state he seldom showed his face without feeling a strong sense of shame. Besides, he had never in his whole life had any interest in study, and so, in the end, he gave up the idea of attending a university.

Once he had openly declared his academic career to be over, the scion of a wealthy family had but one thing to which to devote himself. At once he plunged with abandon into drinking and womanizing, two skills he had been cultivating for some time.

From Master Yun's point of view, it was bad enough to have a grandson who had succumbed to vice so young and who seemed destined to remain a nonentity; it was still worse for him to watch his precious money being squandered by his grandson as if it were water; and worst of all, the old man saw his grand dream of having a county magistrate in the family drifting away like a little frog caught in summer floodwaters.

Master Yun, however, was not the sort of man who abandons his high hopes at the first setback. Having sought counsel from various people around him and having long brooded over the alternatives, he realized that with the educational route to a magistracy now blocked, he would have to resort to a different strategy. There was another way to the goal, a step-by-step rise through the bureaucracy, starting as a lowly clerk in a county office, then being promoted to chief of the general affairs section, thence to a bureau chief position and, finally, to a magistracy.

Since Master Yun was very close to the magistrate of his hometown, and was also very friendly with the mayor, he arranged for Chongsu to get a clerk's post. Then, depending on how well his behind-the-scenes campaign of support turned out, promotions would follow: "Yes, he'd make a good general affairs bureau chief." "Take it, here's a magistracy." Thus would Chongsu effortlessly climb the ladder to high rank.

Indeed, as matters unfolded, the magistrate back home readily provided Chongsu with a position in the township office, and he also pledged to Master Yun that he would see to Chongsu's future.

Chongsu himself was not that eager to become a magistrate. However, he preferred a carefree life in the country to a life in Seoul under the close supervision of his cheerless grandfather. It was decided that he would receive from home a monthly stipend of two hundred *wŏn* on becoming a clerk, a job paying a monthly salary of twenty six *wŏn*. And he had taken the post, exactly three years earlier.

Over those three years, the amount of money Master Yun had personally disbursed to promote Chongsu's career came to thirteen thousand *wŏn*. In addition, Chongsu had taken another twenty thousand for the stated purpose of promotional entertainment. Heaven only knows how much of that was actually spent in that cause, and how much was siphoned off for other uses. All in all, the total investment actually was a good deal over thirty thousand *wŏn*. Beyond that, Chongsu's monthly allowance came to more than seven thousand *wŏn* over the preceding three years. Then, there were two instances in which Chongsu had forged Master Yun's seal to borrow twenty thousand by mortgaging land, and it cost the old man twenty-five thousand to clear the titles and settle the interest at eight *chŏn* a day. There were also six different occasions when Chongsu generously co-signed promissory notes for his friends' loans, with Master Yun ending up paying another forty thousand to retire those debts.

These escapades involved nearly seventy thousand *wŏn*, but out of that sum the amount actually pocketed by Chongsu for his personal use was less than a total of ten thousand *wŏn*. Viewed from Master Yun's position, he had been swindled by his grandson, so he might have held out and refused payment. Ultimately, however, that would have meant Chongsu going to jail. The old man couldn't allow that to happen, partly out of a need to save face, but more importantly because it would have foreclosed the realization of his lifelong dream, a magistracy in the family.

The thirsty man, they say, digs the well. Similarly, Master Yun was left with no choice but to mop up the messes Chongsu left behind. On those occasions Master Yun, aghast and irate, would summon Chongsu, cursing him with his favorite malediction—"I'll have your balls cut off!" Then the old man would interrogate his grandson like a thief, demanding to know how in the world he had let the money run through his fingers like water.

Invariably Chongsu would reply that he had used the funds to cultivate influence in order to advance his quest for a magistracy. In that case, Master Yun would inquire why had he borrowed from a usurer instead of coming to him for the money. Chongsu would snap back a reminder that his grandfather seldom disbursed money upon request.

Master Yun didn't buy the explanations, of course, but all the same these instances illustrate the kind of leverage Chongsu had acquired over the old man.

Considering the awesome sum, nearly one hundred thousand *wŏn*, that Master Yun himself had poured down the drain in three short years, one can readily imagine the powerful hold the objective of obtaining a magistracy exercised over the old man. To have a so-called aristocrat in the family was an obsession. Chongsu, however, had not made a single step up the bureaucratic ladder; he was still a lowly clerk. His only progress was a raise of three *wŏn*, making his salary twenty-nine *wŏn* a month.

Things being thus convoluted, and progress so negligible, one might suppose that Master Yun, hot-tempered as a rule, would be losing patience. In fact, it was understood from the start that promotion from clerk to general affairs section chief would take four years, the next hop to bureau chief another three years, and then three years more to secure a magistracy. Because it was a ten-year plan, Master Yun was still rather unperturbed in his assessment of Chongsu's climb.

The one who capitalized on this leisurely attitude was Chongsu. His post in the county office was merely a front. His daily routine revolved around drinking and philandering, and he made four or five trips to Seoul each month for the sole purpose of debauchery.

The money for all this was, of course, wheedled from the family. However much he had, and however urgent the outlays he faced, he was always ready to spend whatever money he could lay his hands on. If hard pressed to repay a debt, he soon reverted to his old trick of defrauding the family, or he would go brazenly to Master Yun and ask for money under the pretext of promotional disbursements.

This trip to Seoul was no different. Only a few days

were left before he would have to repay one thousand *wŏn* he had borrowed from another county official. Moreover, the weather was turning cool and he had an irresistible urge to go on a drinking binge. Such were the reasons for his visit to Seoul, but whether he got up on the wrong side of the bed, or just was having an unlucky day, from the moment he got off the train, things had been going from bad to worse.

First, Pyŏngho, the beanpole, had failed to appear at the station to meet him, even though Chongsu had sent him a telegram the day before. Without this lackey, Chongsu was utterly helpless. Without Pyŏngho he couldn't borrow money for a drinking spree or find a woman. Pyŏngho knew how to discount a bill, how to locate the better *kisaeng* houses, how to negotiate a fancy banquet on credit, how to put him in touch with a likely woman, and so on. Consequently, to have a good time in Seoul, Chongsu needed Pyŏngho even more than he needed money.

That was why Chongsu had taken the trouble to send a wire in advance, but when he arrived at Seoul Station, Pyŏngho was nowhere in sight. He must be out of town or maybe ill, Chongsu told himself disappointedly. But just to make sure, he walked all the way to Pyŏngho's house, which clung to the side of a hill in Ahyŏndong.

As expected, Pyŏngho wasn't in. According to his wife, he had gone out the day before, saying he would return shortly, but hadn't yet shown up. Then he must still be in town, Chongsu told himself. Relieved, he asked Pyŏngho's wife to have him get in touch as soon as he came back. Chongsu next went to an inn, where he always stayed when he was in Seoul. He checked into the inn before going to see his family.

Chongsu had breakfast in the inn and then took a long nap. The sleeping cars on the train had been full and he was very tired. He needed plenty of rest to restore his stamina in order to be ready for a wild evening. Without Pyŏngho, Chongsu was like a blind man without his cane, utterly incapable of moving about on his own. So taking a nap was the handiest thing for him to do.

It was after midday when Chongsu woke from his nap. There was still no sign of Pyŏngho, so he went again to the house, but it was no use. Growing desperate, he began to search the city streets. That was when, as bad luck would have it, he had run into Okhwa in front of Umi Hall.

Chongsu returned to the inn and waited until four in the afternoon. He got so sick and tired of waiting that he began thinking halfheartedly he might be better off changing his plans entirely— instead of staying he could try to extort one thousand *wŏn* from his grandfather and head back to the country. Or, he could stay in Seoul for one more day. But who should walk in out of the blue but Pyŏngho, a bovine smile on his long, horsy face.

"Hello! I'm awfully sorry!"

"You've been swilling all night, haven't you, dipping your beak all over the city?" Chongsu said sarcastically without even bothering to get up. He just sat there looking up at Pyŏngho, as if he were peering up at an electric pole. This proclivity to shower others with offensive speech must have been an hereditary trait handed down from Master Yun.

In any event, Chongsu cut the profile of a real bastard. Not only was Pyŏngho from the same hometown, but he was fifteen years Chongsu's senior. That fifteen years made him old enough to be Chongsu's father. In fact, Chongsu's father, Yun Ch'angsik, who was forty-six, was on a first name basis with Pyŏngho. But now, here was Chongsu, sprawled comfortably on the floor, launching an ill-mannered verbal assault on a man he ought to have greeted with the courtesy of a deep bow. What else could one call him, then, but a perfect bastard?

Pyŏngho, however, was not in the least offended.

"Well, I stumbled on a gold mine and it took a while to make the most of it . . ."

"Ah, so you've been out to that villa on the outskirts of the city?"

"Right."

"Had a taste of a girl, eh?"

"You crazy bastard! An old man like me doesn't go aping over young women any more, you know that."

"Sure! A hungry dog will pass by a bone, right?"

The two men traded vulgar jabs. So it was Pyŏngho, after all, and his ready scorn of propriety that accounted for Chongsu's vulgar impertinence. In order to be someone's lackey, and a good one at that, a certain professional indulgence was unavoidable— that was Pyŏngho's excuse.

At last Chongsu raised himself to a squat and lit a cigarette.

"I need some money," he said.

"We'll try . . . how much?"

As always, Pyŏngho's reaction was confident and practical.

"I have to have a thousand at least, and another five hundred . . ."

"Need it today?"

"The thousand can wait until tomorrow afternoon, but I'd like to have the five today."

"I'll do my best! But the banks are closed, it won't be easy."

"If you'd been here at noon there'd be no problem! Instead you've been licking around . . ."

"Lord! What a bastard you are! Would a woman go wash clothes if she knew it'd be raining? Why didn't you send the telegram a few hours earlier?"

"That's enough; cut out the chatter! Hurry up; figure something out!"

"No good rushing me, hurry up and fill that out."

Chongsu was filling out a promissory note for discount, saying as he wrote,

"This time . . . this time I better use my own seal, even if it means paying higher interest."

"Why do you want to do that? That'll make things difficult."

"Remember the fifteen thousand I borrowed last time? Well I used my grandfather's seal, pledging his land as security, and the money's due at the end of the month, isn't it?"

"Come to think of it, you're right. But so what?"

"So, if this one surfaces before the other is settled, and if that other one creates a stink, well, I'm having a hard enough time dealing with one at a time, so how can I justify two at the same time?"

Chongsu lifted his fountain pen from the paper and shook his head repeatedly, his tongue darting in and out. The hard time he expected would not be from creditors but from his grandfather, Master Yun.

"Don't you see? It's worth enduring that ordeal for a large sum, but to be ground up and spit out for two thousand in petty cash is ludicrous!"

"Got a point there, but still . . ."

Pyŏngho, pensively blinking his eyes, took the two-thousand-*wŏn* note once Chongsu had put his seal on it. To borrow money on the unsecured promise of Yun Chongsu, a dissolute grandson, without a guarantee from Master Yun, at least a forged one, would be about as easy as plucking a star from the sky.

"It'll be a little difficult," Pyŏngho said, smacking his lips and swaying to and fro as he fingered the note.

"Would I have waited for you all day if it was going to be easy? Enough talk! Go on now, give it a try. And hurry back!"

"Well, I'll do what I can, but . . ."

Pyŏngho rose and put the note in the inner pocket of his faded gray jacket.

"I'll see what I can do with this. If it doesn't work out, we'll just have to think of another way . . . anyhow, you wait here for me . . ."

"I need that money! For tonight, especially, I must have four, five hundred *wŏn.*"

"Must? You mean for this?"

Grinning broadly, Pyŏngho made a motion of pouring wine. Chongsu smiled back.

"A sparrow never passes a mill, eh?"

"Don't worry. If I don't get the cash, we can always drink on credit."

"No, no credit. Besides, there'd be no money for the *kisaeng* house."

"I can get you a woman on credit, too, you know."

"What sort of shameless bastard would take a woman on credit!"

"I would, if I could."

"That's the difference between aristocrats and commoners, isn't it?"

"I don't see the highborn doing any different."

In the end Pyŏngho left, saying he'd be back within

an hour. Chongsu waited. Two hours passed, then three, and his eyes were about to pop out. When Pyŏngho finally showed up at seven-thirty he was emptyhanded. There was only one man, he said, who would lend money to Chongsu without Master Yun's guaranty, and his checks were as good as cash, accepted everywhere. Pyŏngho had combed half the city in search of this man, but he couldn't find him anywhere.

Chongsu had no way of knowing that this story was a sly scheme Pyŏngho had concocted on the spur of the moment. The moneylender mindless enough to cash one of Chongsu's drafts had not been born yet. Pyŏngho was well aware of this, of course, but his greed led him to pretend there was some possibility. He wanted Chongsu to draw up a note— it might come in handy someday, one never knew. Chongsu would remain eternally ignorant of the fact that for the past three hours Pyŏngho had not been wandering the city in search of anyone but rather lying comfortably at home.

"Damn! What can I do now?"

His irritation building, Chongsu savagely crushed his lit cigarette into the ashtray. Then he launched into a diatribe against Pyŏngho for returning so late.

"Damn it! If I'd known it'd turn out this way, I could've gone home before sunset and talked to my grandfather."

Chongsu's lament, however, was music to the ears of Pyŏngho, who was secretly applauding the twists and turns of events.

"Tell you what, Chongsu. Why don't you put your grandfather's seal right there, and I'll give it another go."

"No, I better not! Never mind, I'll just go tomorrow and ask my grandfather for a thousand *wŏn*."

"You don't really think he'll give it to you, do you?"

"If he doesn't, well, that's that! Damn!"

"If it makes no difference, why are you so eager to get the money?"

"Don't be such a smart aleck. That thousand *wŏn* is about to put several families in mourning . . . you don't understand."

"You're right, I don't."

"If this draft is endorsed with my grandfather's seal, can you get me the cash right away?"

"Seven chances out of ten, I can, but listen . . ."

"All right. Let's hear it."

"You say you'll be in deep trouble if you don't get the money from your grandfather, right?"

"It's not just trouble . . . never in my life have I needed a lousy thousand *wŏn* so badly!"

"That's why I'm telling you to put your grandfather's seal on the draft, and I'll go out right away and see what I can do. If I fail, I can try again tomorrow. Meanwhile, don't rely totally on me. Go and see your grandfather. Press him. That way if one or the other plan works out, you'll be in good shape, right?"

"Listen to him!"

Chongsu pointed his finger at Pyŏngho and abruptly sat up, irritated at the misunderstanding.

"You obviously weren't listening to what I said before!" he continued in an excited tone.

"Yes, I was! You said it wouldn't do because the prior loan, the fifteen thousand secured by land, and this one will have to be paid off one right after the other, isn't that right?"

"And I have a feeling my grandfather might hear about this one first— that's what worries me most right now!"

"Well, I've got an idea. Why don't you extend the due

date for this one, say, twice or three times, and just pay the interest in the meantime?"

"Extend the due date? Who'd allow such a thing?"

"Why wouldn't they? No reason not to, as long as you pay the interest."

"Well, shall I try it then? Heh, heh . . ."

Chongsu suddenly emitted an insipid laugh as he took out his grandfather's seal— he never failed to carry it with him— and stamped the draft. Then watching Pyŏngho put on his shoes, he asked imploringly,

"Do bring some of it in cash, even if it's only a hundred *wŏn*, won't you?"

"Well, I'll see what I can do, but . . ."

Pyŏngho started to turn away, but paused, smiling broadly, and added, "Say, how about trying a schoolgirl for a change this evening, instead of the usual *kisaeng?*"

"A schoolgirl? Stop talking nonsense!"

"No! Upon my word, I can bring one for sure . . ."

"The real thing?"

"Naturally!"

"You mean it?"

"Trust me!"

"What if she's not?"

"You can behead me!"

"All right, it's a bet?"

"You're on! I lose my head if she's a fake, but what do I get if she's real?"

"You'll get a reward of one hundred *wŏn!*"

"Good, I'll put in an order on my way back."

Within an hour Pyŏngho was back, but once again his efforts had been fruitless. He had made three different calls, all regular contacts, but one was out of town, another out on the town, and the third had no funds on deposit at the moment and said he would have to go to the bank the next day to arrange for an overdraft.

Of course, this too was a story Pyŏngho had fabricated. Actually, he had spent the time chit-chatting with a pimp in the red-light district of Tonggwan.

Contrary to Pyŏngho's expectation, however, Chongsu showed no trace of impatience.

"Then you should be able to get the money by tomorrow?"

"Well, we'll see . . ."

"You're not sure?"

"I'll tell you what. Leave the draft with me and I'll make another round. But to be safe, do your best to get the money from your grandfather . . . that's the sure and safe way. If you rely only on me and my efforts fail, there will surely be a huge mess. You see what I'm saying? On my way back just now I gave this a lot of thought, and I assure you it's no easy matter to lay hands on money tucked away in somebody else's pocket. The slightest slip and you can bungle a matter of the greatest importance! Take tonight, for instance. We've been depending on other people's money and so we end up facing failure after failure, you see?"

Chongsu kept nodding his head at these persuasive words of wisdom from Pyŏngho. And with Chongsu so attentive, Pyŏngho was secretly overjoyed, for his plan appeared headed for success— nine chances out of ten he would succeed.

Pyŏngho had no intention of ever giving the draft back. If Chongsu got the money from his grandfather, he would have no use for the draft. Most likely he would forget about it and just head back home to the countryside. If, by any chance, he remembered and asked for it, Pyŏngho could always come up with an excuse, like, "Oh, dear! Last night in the outhouse there was no paper . . ."

If, on the other hand, Chongsu failed to get the money from Master Yun and needed to cash the draft, Pyŏngho meant to give him the same excuse and make him draw up another. So, either way, Pyŏngho meant to keep the draft for himself, and in good time to swallow the proceeds, seventeen hundred *wŏn,* after deducting the fifteen percent advance interest.

This planned feast would bring no unsavory aftermath, he knew. In the first place, from a legal point of view, Pyŏngho was guilty of nothing. In any case, the matter would never grow into anything so grandiose. Sooner or later, the draft would find its way into Master Yun's hands, and no doubt Chongsu would be badly mauled. Chongsu would figure out immediately who was responsible for the fraud. But being a softhearted man, he would keep his lips sealed and shoulder the blame himself, rather than expose the sordid details to the light of day.

Chongsu would probably make some impertinent remark about it later— that he'd consider the money had been spent for dressing up his stepchild— but he would still keep Pyŏngho on as his trusted lackey, partly because he never held a grudge against anybody, but more because Pyŏngho had become indispensable to him.

All Pyŏngho had to do was take the matter in hand before it exploded, imploring mercy from Chongsu with the right sort of plea, such as, "Why, my dear Chongsu, something entirely unexpected came up, a matter of life and death, so I took the liberty of using your draft for this or that purpose. Do as you like with me, now. Kill me if you wish." Then, Chongsu, being Chongsu, would accept the explanation as sincere, and out of pity he might even have a couple of new suits made for Pyŏngho.

"Now, hurry up and get dressed. Let's be off!" Pyŏngho urged Chongsu, smiling all the while from the excitement of having already mentally devoured seventeen hundred *wŏn.*

"Don't worry about tomorrow until tomorrow is here . . . now, this evening, first you must have some real fun with a fresh young schoolgirl, and then, go to some villa and spend the whole night . . . you know, eh?"

"All talk and no money!"

"Didn't I say not to worry? I'll see to it that the expenses at the villa will be on credit, and ten *wŏn* will be more than enough for the schoolgirl!"

"Ten *wŏn!*"

"Sure! How much cash do you have on you now?"

"About thirty, but . . ."

"Good! Ten *wŏn* for the price of the girl, and twenty as a tip to the waiters at the villa, why, you've got enough!"

"This schoolgirl you keep talking about, she's not a fake, is she?"

"Never! Didn't I say you can have me beheaded?"

"Still, if ten *wŏn* is enough, that's even cheaper than the going rate in the red-light district."

"Anyway, no point arguing here, you'll see for yourself when we get there, all right?"

Such were the circumstances that brought Chongsu, a man of his time, to a house of ill repute in Tonggwan.

A thirteen-watt bulb hung in a stranglehold from the center of the low ceiling. The rafters, coarsely pasted over with grayish black newspaper, protruded from the ceiling like the ribs of a consumptive. The wallpaper, once white, was discolored to a dingy yellow and, loosened by time, was peeling from the walls here and there. Some splotches of bedbug blood in the shape of bamboo leaves would have made the room picture perfect, but the absence of such bespoke the fact that the room was used not for ordinary habitation but for that particular temporary purpose only.

Folded up in one corner of the room was a set of mats and blankets, pretty much flattened from lack of repadding despite years of hard use. The dank smell of mildew was so thick in the room that it completely enveloped you from the instant you entered. The sole piece of furniture was a chipped ashtray. Chongsu and Pyŏngho sat with the ashtray between them, mechanically smoking. At last, Chongsu took a long look around the room, the same frown on the bridge of his nose as when he had first set foot in the place. In a lowered voice, he reproached Pyŏngho,

"This is nothing but a common whorehouse. I see no difference, do you? You and your stories, I never should have . . ."

"Well, it's a brothel all right, but things are different these days!"

"Some difference! Listen, I've been frequenting these places since I was eighteen, so keep in mind that you're not speaking to an amateur!"

"In the old days there was only one kind of woman here, but these days the selection is unbelievable! If you ask for a schoolgirl, they bring you a schoolgirl. If you ask for a widow, a widow is escorted in. Concubine, housewife, busgirl, actress, salesgirl, and so on and so forth. You name it, that's what you get!"

"There you go again with your foolishness! How can a widow prove she's really a widow? Is she going to bring her family register with her? Do the schoolgirls show up with student I.D.s? And the busgirls wear coin-changers, I suppose?"

"Of course not; it's not done that way," Pyŏngho said with a laugh. "Still," he continued, "you usually get what you're looking for. You know, what with this sort of variety, nowadays they don't call the place a brothel anymore, they call it a universal trading company!"

"What nonsense! You don't even know the story behind the name 'universal trading company,' do you?"

A few years earlier there had been an incident when the police conducted a surprise raid on a den of pimps. A few dozen conspirators were arrested, and in the course of the investigation the authorities were greatly surprised not only by the sophisticated structure of the organization, but even more by its front name, "Universal Trading Company." There was no special significance to this name, of course. In all probability the only intention of the proprietors in choosing this absurd tradename had been to evade the suspicions of the authorities.

At any rate, since that episode it had become usual for all brothels to be referred to as the universal trading company. The name was quite widely adopted in subterranean circles. After listening to Chongsu's account of the history of the name, Pyŏngho rose with a smile on his face.

"Well, well," he said, "you're far more knowledgeable than me, that's for certain! And now, I'd better go ahead . . ."

"Go where?"

"Go on to the villa to make some arrangements. I'll be waiting for you there. Take your time and have some fun."

"That's not really necessary, is it? Now that we're

here, why don't we call for two and the two of us together . . . what do you say?" Chongsu suggested with a
chuckle.

"Don't tease an old man," Pyŏngho responded with a
giggle, "and by the way, with regard to the tab here,
never mind the food and what not, just put a ten *wŏn*
note in the old lady's palm on your way out."

"O.K. But if the schoolgirl turns out to be fake, you'll
lose your head! I mean it!"

"Don't worry!"

Once out in the hall, Pyŏngho summoned the old
woman and whispered a word or two into her ear before
he walked out.

Chongsu took out his pocket watch. He peered at the
hands, which showed nine-twenty. The old woman
stealthily slid open the sliding door and stuck her pock-
marked face into the room. A long pipe was clenched in
her teeth.

"You must be feeling bored since the other gentleman
left," the old woman said, whereupon she walked into
the room with her arms crossed and sat down where
Pyŏngho had been.

"My! What a handsome face you have!" she continued. "The girl will be here soon. One look at you and
she'll fall head over heels for you!"

Her glib tongue befit her profession as a madam, and
the sound of her affected laughter was almost too loathsome to bear.

"This girl who's coming, is she really a schoolgirl?"
Chongsu asked, striking up a conversation. He was
curious what her reply would be.

"Certainly! A genuine schoolgirl! A real high school
student! You might think I'd bring you a fake schoolgirl,
a woman dressed up in a student's uniform, but times

have changed and we can't afford to deceive our customers. Of course she's a real schoolgirl!"

"How come a real student doesn't stick to her studies like she ought to?"

"My, my! You don't think schoolgirls don't know what they want, do you? Well, they do, all of them. Some girls come here out of boredom, and those who've had a taste of money come for money . . . but the girl coming now, she's not the sort who's only after money or out to kill boredom! You must keep that in mind, sir, and please don't treat her too roughly! Otherwise . . ."

"What, then, is she coming for?"

"A husband! She's looking for a husband. The ideal husband!"

"Indeed! Hmm, looking for a husband!"

"Why, she's a rare beauty. Not a single blemish!"

"Really? That beautiful?"

"Don't say another word! You'll fall in love with her at first sight. You'll be begging her to marry you tomorrow! You never know," the madam added with an affected laugh.

"Not a bad idea if we hit it off," Chongsu said. "I've been thinking of getting married, so . . ."

"If that's what you have in mind, sir, don't spare the money. Be generous, show her you can spend twenty or thirty *wŏn* tonight! Then she'll get the idea . . ."

"But I thought you said this one wasn't after money?"

"Why, no, she's not, not for now, but she needs to know her future husband is well-off and generous. That'll make her be more drawn to you, see what I mean?"

"You've got a point there! How old is she?"

"Goodness! There's no need to be so impatient, she'll be here any minute now. You're all primed in advance, aren't you? She's just turned nineteen this year. A perfect age!"

At that moment from outside came the creaking sound of the gate swinging open, followed by light footsteps, and then a cautious voice called out, "Anybody in?"

Already on her feet, the old woman was about to leave through the side door, but she turned around and winked at Chongsu.

"She's here!"

In spite of himself, Chongsu felt tense. He strained to hear the goings-on outside. At first he hadn't given much credence to the old lady's rigamarole, and he had told himself that the girl would very likely turn out to be a fake. All the same, he couldn't help feeling a bit mesmerized, because through all his countless contacts with women of the night, he had never crossed paths with a schoolgirl.

Outside, the old woman spent some time talking in a muffled voice. At last the side door opened again.

"Now, see for yourself if what I told you isn't true! I've brought you a genuine schoolgirl, genuine and respectful!" the old woman said in a confident tone, blocking his view of the girl. Then she stepped aside and made another animated speech, this time to the girl.

"Now, now, come right in, dear! There's nothing to be so bashful about. Such shyness! This here is a modern gentleman, a man of the new age. Hurry in now . . ."

Confronted with this scene, even Chongsu, veteran of over a decade of experience in that world, couldn't help but feel rather overwhelmed, and lacking the guts to stare the girl in the face at the outset, his eyes began from the silk-wrapped feet stepping over the threshold and wandered slowly upward from there.

A plump pair of legs in yellow silk stockings, a thin black voile skirt hanging halfway down those legs, the hands lightly pressing the gathered pleats, a traditional white blouse with the front nicely trimmed, a bow neatly tied on the swells of the breasts . . . scanning slowly upward, Chongsu gradually sank into a solemn mood, anticipating that he would soon experience that symbol of purity, a schoolgirl. But just as Chongsu's glance was about to shift from the girl's roundish chin to her full face, she turned to look at him, and thus came the moment when the two of them saw each other face to face!

"Whhhaat!"

"Good god!"

Neither dared scream; they were both too shocked to breathe. Chongsu almost fell over backward; he barely managed to keep his balance. The girl instantly flew out into the hall and bolted for the gate—with or without her shoes was not clear. The next moment there was utter silence.

After the girl had taken flight, Chongsu pulled himself together and took his leave of the Universal Trade Company. The girl was Okhwa, the second concubine of his own father, Yun Ch'angsik.

Chongsu took a taxi to the villa in the outskirts of the city, feeling very grateful that humans had lights to pierce the darkness of night.

Pyŏngho was sitting all alone; the *kisaeng* had not come out yet. He found Chongsu's unexpectedly early arrival most curious and kept pestering him with questions. Bursting with rage and in search of a target on which to vent his fury, Chongsu felt like pouring his anger on Pyŏngho, demanding that he forfeit his head. But, thinking a tirade would only make things more awkward, Chongsu told him he had received a message that the girl had taken ill suddenly and couldn't come, and since he wasn't feeling too excited about the prospect anyway, he had just gotten up and walked out of the place. It was very like Chongsu to resort to such a story.

Though the Ax Handle Rot . . .
(Or, Latter-day Immortals at Play)

The scene was the sitting room of the residence of Yun Ch'angsik's first concubine in Tongdaemun, the time about nine o'clock that same night.

The main gate, the front door, and the door of the sitting room were all locked tight. The nephew of one of the old servants, a burly, fearsome-looking young man, stood on guard in the servants' quarters to exercise strict control over anyone coming to or going from the house.

A mahjong game, on a grand scale, was in progress. The game had been "on" since the previous night and still seemed far from over.

Ten *chŏn* a point and five hundred *wŏn* a game were the stakes; these players were not gambling for peanuts. Accordingly, locking the gates was not a bad idea. As a rule, however, games attract freeloaders, and this one was no exception. The players had been joined by a half-dozen onlookers, some of whom were hoping for a little victory gift from the big winner. But by this time only a couple of them were still looking over the shoulders of the players; the others were sprawled asleep in the adjoining servants' room, exhausted after twenty-four hours.

Piled high on the shelves around the spacious wood-walled room were old, tattered volumes of the Chinese classics. In one corner stood a glass cabinet in which Koryŏ dynasty white celadon was displayed; and a beautiful twelve-stringed *kayagŭm** leaning against the cabinet added a touch of elegance to the scene.

Hanging here and there on the wall were pieces of calligraphy, white etched on black panels, by the great Yi dynasty master Ch'usa.** Hung on the pillar was a quiver of arrows. Another corner was heaped with dirty dishes and empty bottles from a Chinese restaurant, a scene which bespoke the indolence of the servants of the house.

The walls of the room were double-papered and sprayed with a white powder, so they were literally white-powdered walls. Hanging in a well-proportioned array on one wall were a scroll and paintings of the Four Gracious Gentlemen, plum, orchid, chrysanthemum, and bamboo, by Misan.** Also attracting attention was a scroll of Peonies by Soch'i** which hung above an ornamental table on top of which lay several volumes of the Chinese classics.

The appreciation of Soch'i Peonies suggested that the owner of the room must have been possessed of rather uncommon aesthetic taste, but considering his absorption with gambling, he could only be a worldly minded man of vulgar inclinations. Yet, doing just as he liked, whenever and however he liked, was precisely the pastime most cherished by Yun Ch'angsik. It was a hobby befitting a life sunk in ennui. . . .

There were three mahjong players: Yun Ch'angsik,

---

*See glossary.
**See glossary under ''Ch'usa.''

the man of the house; Fatty Pak, a rich man and excellent at mahjong; and a harelip who was a professional gambler. All three had the same bloodshot eyes, glazed over from lack of sleep, and all three faces had an oily shine.

Yun was leading. In his hand he held a Tonze flush, having begun by playing a pair of eights in Tonze as his head. He was holding two straights: one-two-three and six-seven-eight, and he was aiming to fill two more on the outside, holding a four-five and a seven-eight, plus a single nine in Mienze. At this juncture, therefore, almost any tile in Tonze in combination with anything good on the fourteenth and last draw would guarantee a win. If, for example, he drew a six, it would mean that he would win the game with a three, six, or nine on the final draw. What's more, if he drew a nine he would fill a royal straight flush, the highest possible score, and his points for the whole game would be doubled.

Already five thousand in the hole, and left with an odd single tile worth a hundred points, Yun was in a predicament in which a royal flush would be most welcome. And now, with a little luck, if he could make a perfect hand, he would win four thousand and be almost back to where he started. On the other hand, if either of the other players went out first, Yun would be the big loser again.

As a matter of fact, Yun had lost three thousand *wŏn* since the game started the night before, and if he lost again now, he would be down only another five hundred, so it wasn't so much the money that made him anxious; it was more his eagerness to see that rare, perfect hand come up.

All three players seemed on the verge of going out, and Fatty Pak, breathing heavily, drew a tile from the pool. A six. He showed it off, teasing Yun,

"Heh, heh, it's a snake tile, dangerous. With this you'd be ready to go out, right, Ch'angsik?"

True, if only Pak discarded it, Yun would snatch it up for a four-five-six, and with the six and nine he would need only one more draw to win. But Fatty Pak was a mahjong wizard, and he held on to the six, discarding instead a seven in Mienze, breaking up his five-seven-eight in that suit.

"If you don't give it to me, I'll just have to draw one!"

Yun drew an eight. As he fingered the tile, pondering what to do with it, one of the freeloaders who had been looking over his shoulder gave him a nudge. He was hinting that Yun ought to break up his six-seven-eight and go instead for a four-five-six. That way he could use the pair of sevens for his head, make a four-of-a-kind in eights, and with the remaining eight-nine in Mienze, he could draw for a seven to complete the straight. Or, if he drew another eight, he could move one eight from his four-of-a-kind and make two sets of three instead. Well, Yun was not at all unaware of that strategy. If he chose that route, he might win, but only at the cost of abandoning his quest for a perfect hand. For Yun, given his natural temperament, to abandon that hope was not only beneath his dignity, it would be a betrayal of the lofty ideals of mahjong sportsmanship.

As Yun ungrudgingly discarded the eight, Fatty Pak leapt up in dismay; he could have raised his points with that eight, if only he had not broken up his six-seven-eight.

"I'll take it!" said the harelip gambler, whose turn followed Yun's. He picked it up and placed it with his six and seven. This move was applauded by the harelip's financier, who had been observing the whole proceedings from behind. The harelip knew Yun was aiming for a royal flush, so he was rushing to go out as soon as possible.

Discarding the same tile in Zepai he had drawn for the fourth time, Fatty Pak said,

"Here, Ch'angsik, take this . . ."

"How could you possibly part with such a precious piece?" Yun said as he drew a new tile from the pool. It was a Tonze with three little circles on the face! With a three-four-five completed, all he needed now was to work on the six and nine.

Feeling rather relieved, Yun was about to discard the nine when Min, the senior servant, walked in much agitated, a telegram in his hand. Those absorbed in the game took no notice of it, but the telegram had been brought inside by the gatekeeper some time before and Min had been busy translating the contents into Korean and Chinese characters.

"A telegram for you, sir!"

Totally enthralled by the game, Yun didn't even hear Min. He proceeded to discard the nine.

"That's it!" the harelip gambler exclaimed instantly.

Once more Min repeated,

"A telegram, sir!"

But Yun merely said,

"Uhm, a telegram . . . ? You've got nine and what else? Let's see them, show us!"

"A telegram from Tokyo, sir!"

"From Tokyo? I see."

Yun held out his hand, took the telegram and crumpled it into his vest pocket. Then he waited impatiently for Fatty Pak to take his turn so he could try a draw from the pool.

"Read the telegram, please!"

"Uhm, I will. Has it been translated?"

"Yes, sir."

Fingering the tile he had just drawn, Yun again forgot the telegram. It was a four in Mienze. Yun knew that Fatty Pak had broken up his set, but the harelip had been waiting for that four.

"The telegram, sir, it's urgent!"

"Uhm. Uhm . . . I can't discard this! What's it about?"

"Open it yourself, sir!"

"Uhm, I will . . . if I give this away, I'll be doing our friend a favor . . . what's it about? Is Chonghak ill?"

"No, sir!"

"What, then? Wait a minute, what am I to do with this? Let me read the telegram first. A snake tile, that's what this is! A snake tile, I say!"

Were he to discard that four, the harelip would raise his points and go out. And that meant that his perfect hand would melt into foam. Hence, it wasn't out of interest in the message that he turned to the telegram, but to buy some time to think about his play. Yun's attention remained riveted on the mahjong table as his fingers fumbled in the pocket of his vest for the telegram.

"Hmm, I fear this four in Mienze will be a real troublemaker!"

"Look, friend, the table will be covered in dust before you get around to playing."

"Wait a bit. Let me take a look at this telegram first . . ."

It was only after some more musing and rummaging around that Yun finally unfolded the telegram in his left hand. Thirteen words in translation didn't take much time or effort.

"The bloody bastard!"

An awful frown on his brow, Yun crumpled the telegram and shoved it back into his pocket. Then he banged down the four in Mienze he had found it so hard to part with.

"Goddamn it, I don't care!"

"That's it! That's the one!"

Sure enough, the harelip had been waiting for that four in Mienze.

"That bloody bastard!"

Once more Yun cursed his son Chonghak, on account of the telegram. Although the first curse had been rightfully directed at the contents of the telegram, the second, despite everything, came across as an outburst of anger at having lost the chance for a perfect hand.

In the end the game was lost and Yun was in the hole another five hundred *wŏn*. As Yun busied himself gathering the mahjong tiles for the start of another game, Min asked in a worried voice,

"Shouldn't we notify your father?"

"My father? Well, let me see. . . ."

Yun's reply was halfhearted. He looked down eagerly at the dice he had just thrown.

"Shall I go, sir?"

"You? Well, what's that? Four. I go first . . . so, you'll go yourself, you say?"

"Yes, sir."

"A seven. . . that's all right, too . . . a nine, seven and nine is sixteen . . ."

"Shall I leave now, sir?"

"Well, let me think . . . this is starting out as a rotten hand! As it is, I'll be glad to get back what I've lost in the last seven games . . . I should be the one going . . . if I send you, he'll send for me right away, so . . . *Nokpal* in Zepai, out you go. . . . No wonder I sensed something strange about the bastard! The bloody bastard!"

"Shall I call a taxi, sir?"

"All right."

"You can't leave now; you've just started a new game," Fatty Pak admonished Yun.

"You're right . . . what should I do? Here's a South Wind tile!"

"And here's an East Wind, help yourself!"

"Not me!

Once again Yun Ch'angsik buried himself in the mahjong game. Min, sick and tired, gave up and returned to his room.

Thus, September 10, in the Year of the Ox, was withdrawing into the depths of night, having given everyone — Master Yun, his daughter-in-law, the Seoul Mistress, T'aesik, Yun Ch'angsik, Okhwa, and all the others— their own differently cut slice of life. Soon a new day would break, and we wonder what sort of life that new day has in store for them, and what might be the contents of that telegram from Tokyo. At any rate, the new day will reveal the nature of all these things.

The Sun Sets on the Great Wall

If the new day brings nothing new, if it merely replays what transpired yesterday, we all feel a sense of suffocation and misery. But today is at once the same and yet a day removed from yesterday. And this goes on and on, till a man's hair turns white, and the white head is laid in the grave. . . . Endless though the process may be, somehow man finds each day more fascinating than the day preceding.

A milky lightening of the sky heralded the new day for which we so ardently longed. As day broke the clock struck six, and at the sound Master Yun coughed and awoke to greet another morning. To rise at six sharp was a habit Master Yun zealously observed, a habit unbroken for the past fifty years.

On opening his eyes, the first thing Master Yun did was to take the brass chamber pot and relieve himself of the toxins filtered from his blood in the course of the night. A new day discharges the residue of the old in order to take in new things, furnishing energy for a new life— it's called "metabolism." The discharge of the old! A truly wonderful thing!

Shish, shish. . . . Master Yun cupped his hands together and scooped part of the spurting liquid to his eyes, rinsing them with it over and over. From ancient times washing one's eyes with morning urine has been known as a method for preventing one's eyesight from growing weak. Such was the health regimen Master Yun was practicing.

For thirty years he had religiously followed this practice. Had he caught gonorrhea no doubt he would have gone blind long ago but luckily he had never suffered from that particular malady, and his vision was actually so good that, unless the letters were awfully small, he could still read without difficulty. Whether he owed his good vision to urine eye rinses, well, that was hard to say with any certainty.

Anyone at a loss for an academic research topic might well look into this question: a dissertation on "The Theory of Urine as a Presbyopia Preventative" could easily be worth a Ph.D.

Having completed his vision preservation regimen, one sure to make eyedrop sellers weep, Master Yun changed out of his nightclothes into regular attire. Then he filled his long pipe with tobacco and lit it.

Clouds of smoke gradually filled the brightly lit room. No voice, no sound; he was the only life form in the room, but somehow the inanimate objects seemed more afflicted by boredom than the man himself.

When the pipe was half smoked, Samnam came in, his bushy head slightly tilted to one side as he tried to get his crossed eyes into some semblance of focus. In his hands he held a flask carefully.

As this, too, was part of the morning routine, Samnam quietly presented the flask to Master Yun, who took it without a word. Then, removing the pipe from his mouth, he went to the drawer of a little table and took out a cup made from a seashell.

Drip, drip, drip. The steaming, yellowish liquid, reminding one of nicely warmed *chŏngjong* wine, he poured carefully into the cup until it reached the brim. This, too, was urine. It was no ordinary urine, however. It was the urine of a child, a child young enough to be innocent of the difference between yin and yang, a child still ignorant of the sexual duality of being.

That a child's urine is a health elixir is a belief as ancient as the secret medical lore enjoining urine eye rinses to preserve vision. Keep this in mind; recent talk about scientists somewhere or other extracting some hormone from urine might turn out, after all, to be more than absurd nonsense. And if so, the honor of having discovered the medical hormone in urine should justly be credited to our Korean ancestors.

Thus Master Yun had been utilizing urine in various ways, and this practice of drinking urine had first begun along with the vision regimen some thirty years before. Back in the country, it used to be easy to get the urine of a child, but since moving to Seoul where, as Master Yun put it, "big city people are lacking in benevolence," he had had to pay to maintain his habit.

After some inquiries in the neighborhood, Master Yun had found a poor family with a little child. He promptly made an exclusive contract with this family to deliver the child's urine, always the first urine expelled in the morning after the child awoke. The price was twenty *chŏn* a month . . . the family had asked for thirty, Taebok had counteroffered ten, and in the end they had struck a deal at twenty.

The exclusive urine supply contract once concluded, Samnam, flask slung on his shoulder, was dispatched every day at dawn to collect the goods, and this was the urine brought in to Master Yun on this particular morning.

As Master Yun busied himself pouring the elixir from the flask into his cup, Samnam was preoccupied with peeling a ginger root. As if downing some thick rice wine to wash away a hangover from the night before, Master Yun gulped down a cup of urine, smacked his lips, drank a second cup, and finally a third. When he finished the third cup, Samnam presented him with the ginger root.

"That little son of a bitch must have eaten something salty last night! That's why this stuff tastes so salty!"

Master Yun frowned as he nibbled the ginger.

By nature urine is supposed to be rather salty, but the sophisticated human palate is such a wondrous thing that Master Yun, after thirty years of religious consumption of urine, had by this time acquired the ability to gauge even minute differences in the degree of salinity of urine.

"That little son of a bitch must have downed a whole bowl of soy sauce!"

"Shall I go and tell them from today not to feed the boy soy sauce a bowl at a time, sir?"

For Samnam, it was no small matter that the boy's urine was too salty for the taste of his honorable old master.

"Don't talk nonsense! Who asked you to interfere in the first place?"

"Yes, sir. I won't talk nonsense, sir!"

"You're really hopeless!"

"Yes, sir!"

Samnam picked up the flask and the cup to clean them.

"My Chinese medicine, is it almost ready?"

"Yes, sir."

"Be very careful with it! Yesterday morning it was boiled too long!"

"Yes, sir."

Once Samnam was gone, Master Yun commenced his morning calisthenics. Both legs stretched all the way out, both arms held straight up— this was the get-ready posture. Then the upper body and the two extended arms were suddenly bent forward, hands aimed down at the toes, as if to grab them, only to rebound immediately. Then, another bend and another stretch, over and over again. . . .

Bending and unbending repeatedly, not at all an easy task for a corpulent man with a big belly, Master Yun counted out "one, two, three . . ." until he reached fifty. By that time, sure enough, what at the outset had seemed physically impossible had become a reality— the tips of his fingers finally touched the tips of his toes.

This might strike one as a rather simple method of increasing stamina. Some may argue that radio calisthenics would have been better suited to the goal. But while radio calisthenics were suitable for the young, they would have been too unseemly for a dignified old man like Master Yun.

Drenched in sweat and slightly out of breath, Master Yun sat in front of the wide open window and enjoyed the cool early morning breeze. It was quite bright outside, and already a sting of coldness was detectable in the wind.

"Some weather!" he muttered to himself in dismay, at which point Taebok came in for his usual morning greeting and to consult about the business agenda for the day.

"This cold weather is going to be big trouble for us!" Deprived of the chance to say "Good morning," Taebok knelt humbly on the floor.

"I see what you mean, sir," he said. "If this continues

and there is an early frost, it will be bad for us."

"That's precisely what I'm saying! What's God got against me anyway! Good God, I wonder! Frost is one thing, but in this kind of weather the rice will never be ripe by harvest time! I've got problems enough as it is, you know. My sharecroppers have started pestering me to death, demanding rent reductions, all thanks to that bloody flood!"

Since the beginning of autumn, the harvest had been a constant worry for both Master Yun and Taebok. Throughout the nation it had generally been a bountiful year, except for some flood damage in Chŏlla Province, where some of Master Yun's ricefields were located. In some paddies, barely half the normal harvest would be salvageable, and others had been so completely swamped that he would have to hire an army of labor-ers to rebuild the dikes. In fact he wouldn't get a single grain of rice from them.

Taebok had gone down to the country about a month and a half earlier to see the situation with his own eyes, and he found the dismal reports from the tenants were not exaggerated.

All the same, Master Yun was not lacking in excuses for merciless intransigence. His argument went some-thing like this: A natural disaster has nothing whatever to do with his tenants because, under their contracts, they had to pay their rents in advance. It was all spelled out in the contracts, so whether there was a poor harvest, or no harvest at all, the rents had to be paid in advance. It was only fair that the farmers pay rents as prescribed in their contracts, wasn't it? If, for instance, I'm supposed to reduce the rents in bad years, would I then be able to demand increased rents when there's a bumper harvest? If I tried to increase the

rent beyond the originally agreed rate, would my tenants consent? They'd refuse, of course. Consequently,
their attempts to use a poor harvest as a pretext for
rent reduction are senseless, unfounded demands!

It was ironclad logic, indeed. Moreover, according to
Master Yun's reasoning, the enlightenment of the modern age had made the world a better place to live, but
too much of that damned enlightenment brings more
harm than good. It led to utterly useless laws such as
the so-called regulations on the use of farmland, and
the controls on tenancy relations, which only encouraged sharecropping bastards to grow more and more
impertinent by demanding unbearable reductions of
annual rents, or pressing the landlords not to raise
rents, or prohibiting the arbitrary transfer of tenants,
and so on and so forth.

All these developments made Master Yun sick to his
stomach. It was simply beyond his comprehension that
he could not control the rents on his own land and that
he could no longer shuffle tenants as he pleased but
had to endure interference by the county office and the
district government, not to mention the police. Tenants'
complaints aside, then, the whole situation was too
great a riddle for Master Yun to solve.

In all events, it looked as though at least a thousand
bags of rice would be lost due to the flood. Master Yun
was resolved to stand firm, of course, but he couldn't
act against the counsel or the orders of the local government or the police. Of late, then, whenever the master and his clerk had a chance to sit down face-to-face,
this situation had been their major worry. They racked
their brains to come up with a scheme, a scheme suffi-
ciently brilliant to make the tenants relent on their
demands and cough up their rents in full.

And now, as if to aggravate matters, the unexpected early cold weather cast in doubt any promise of a decent rice harvest.

While Samnam brought in the Chinese medicine, Master Yun was discussing various aspects of these problems with Taebok. The medicine was a restorative herbal brew, with ginseng and deer antlers as its main ingredients. By drinking urine, doing calisthenics, taking Chinese medicine, or any other plausible method, Master Yun was determined to guard his health. To live a long, long life was his sole desire.

Glorying in his present wealth, no, by ceaselessly increasing his annual income of ten thousand bags of rice, Master Yun wanted to live to be a hundred, two hundred, a thousand, ten thousand years old, no, to live as long as heaven and earth endure. And heaven and earth would last forever, so he wanted to live eternally, in harmony with the universe. For Master Yun, the mere thought of leaving his wealth behind and parting with such a wonderful world was intolerable.

In ancient times, the Emperor of Qin, anxious for immortality, is said to have sent out five thousand boys and girls to comb the enchanted gardens along the East Sea in search of the mystical herb of immortality. And Master Yun was just as anxious for immortality as the Emperor of Qin.

True enough, Master Yun often said, "Will I live another hundred years, or even fifty? Not at all. I have another ten years, if that, before I die. . . ." This was, of course, no lie, for such are the ways of all mortal souls under heaven, but as far as Master Yun was personally concerned it was mere talk. In his heart of hearts he wanted far more than a miserable ten years of existence; he didn't want to die at all.

Eternal life . . . by any means . . . like the Emperor of Qin, Master Yun desperately longed for a deathless, never-ending life.

Master Yun's unbending struggle to accumulate and to guard his wealth, and his desire to ennoble his family by cultivating a county magistrate and a police chief, were similar in a way to the world-renowned enterprise of the Great Wall, that historical landmark of a project carried out by the Emperor of Qin to protect his dominion from the northern barbarians. In truth, Master Yun's own enterprise, a monumental project spiritually and historically, was in essence no different from the Emperor's Great Wall.

The Emperor of Qin, who built the Great Wall to make his kingdom endure eternally and who sought to bask eternally in imperial glory by eating the mystical herb of immortality, and Master Yun, who devoted himself to the amassing of a family fortune, and to gilding his clan with aristocratic titles, who planned to enjoy eternal glory as the patriarch of the household, and so drank urine, did calisthenics, and ate restorative medicines . . . between these two men no difference could be discerned.

When it was nearly eight o'clock, Master Yun went out to the main room for breakfast, and by the time he returned to his room it was already almost nine.

Not a speck of a cloud occluded the sky, and the sunlight was warm and vibrant. A fair day, indeed, and another happy new day for Master Yun. Sometime that afternoon he would be making one thousand *wŏn* by discounting that seven-thousand-*wŏn* draft for only five thousand nine hundred and fifty. Even after the hundred-and-five-*wŏn* commission to Tadpole, he would still be clearing nine hundred and forty-five *wŏn* in interest.

Hence, it would be a happy day, bringing him a handsome profit.

Also anticipated that day was an interlude of you-know-what with Ch'unsim, so it would be a sort of a luxury special edition of a day.

The other members of the family were also fine, though "happy" or "content" might be words a bit too grand to describe their state of mind.

T'aesik was out in the alley now, gorging himself with toffee, and was thus better than fine. . . .

Kyŏngson, unmindful of his studies, was lost completely in a reverie of the night before, when he had squandered two *wŏn* on a date with Ch'unsim. . . .

Having already assumed a horizontal position on the floor, *Ch'uwŏlsaek* cradled in her hands, the Seoul Mistress was entranced, totally liberated from all worldly cares and sorrows. . . .

At the back of the house, the two sisters-in-law, Kyŏngson's mother and aunt, were absorbed in their sewing, the former feeling much relieved by the prospect that her husband Chongsu would surely be putting in an appearance that day. . . .

Ko, Master Yun's daughter-in-law, who had come home in a drunken stupor after three that morning, was deep in sleep. . . .

At the villa in the outskirts of Tongsomun, Chongsu was in nirvana, a sumptuous table before him, *kisaeng* all around him, and Pyŏngho at his side. . . .

Okhwa was feeling a bit uneasy about the unexpected encounter the night before, but even if it leaked out and brought her relationship with Yun Ch'angsik to an end, she wouldn't be all that sad since she had already gotten a house, jewelry, and several thousand in cash out of him. . . .

Yun Ch'angsik had blown a grand total of four thousand five hundred *wŏn* in the mahjong game, but he didn't give it a second thought since it was less than five thousand. He thought of it as money spent on a drinking binge and went to bed at dawn. At this very moment he was fast asleep, transported far away from any worries about that telegram from Tokyo. . . .

Such was the general state of the Yun family, and now back to the old master himself.

Master Yun reproached himself for having asked Ch'unsim to come so late, around noon. He also was fretful at the possibility she might not show at all since she had been summoned home the night before to attend to her suddenly stricken father. But as the clock struck nine, much to his surprise, Ch'unsim rushed in, breathless and gay.

What a pleasant surprise! Master Yun heaved up and down as if he were about to leap up and dash out the door to meet her. A bright smile beamed over his face.

"Come right in . . . your father, is he feeling better today?"

"Yes, he's quite well now."

Ch'unsim stood on the step outside, showing no intention of entering the room.

"Come on out, please. Let's go buy the ring."

"Heh, heh, heh, my little bitch hasn't forgotten! Very well, let's go! To hell with it!"

"Me? Forget? I haven't slept a wink all night! I came at nine when you told me to come at noon, doesn't that tell you something? Hurry, get dressed, please!"

"All right."

Master Yun staggered to his feet and began to prepare for the outing.

"What if the people at the jewelers think you are a

schoolgirl and speak ill of you for wearing a ring?"

"Who cares what they say? Nothing matters as long as it pleases me."

"Is that a fact? Well, if that's how you feel, I see no problem."

"Of course you don't! Why should you?"

"All right, all right."

His conscience not entirely free of guilt, Master Yun felt like saying something, just to hear his own voice.

Just as he had the day before when he went to the Festival of Great Singers, Master Yun now put a splendid *T'ongyŏng kat* on his head, wore clothes of the finest quality ramie fabric, and on his feet he put white cotton stockings and perfectly fitted black leather shoes. In one hand was his stylish cane with the silver dog handle and in the other his folding fan with thirty-four bamboo ribs.

The couple resembled an enormous steamship accompanied by a tiny toot-toot tug, but at any rate they arrived in due course at the foot of Ch'in Hill. The passersby riveted long, sharp glances on Master Yun, scanning him slowly from head to feet. The Japanese residents in the area, especially, gaped, overwhelmed by the imposing air of nobility exuded by Master Yun as his impressive bulk almost blocked the narrow alleys. They were smitten by his dignified visage and his refined apparel, being used to thinking of Koreans as peddlers in dirty shirts, pants rolled up over bare calves, carrying heavy loads on the A-frame on their shoulders. They were accustomed to seeing Koreans wearing white cotton topcoats, faces clouded, mouths hanging listlessly open as they entered a store quietly and then slipped away stealthily after rummaging for a long time through everything on the shelves.

In a way, therefore, Master Yun compelled the Japanese to recognize that there was nobility in the Koreans, too. He had, in fact, unwittingly conducted a silent protest on behalf of the Korean people, though such was far indeed from what he was of a mind to accomplish.

Ch'unsim, who had been leading the way, halted in front of a jewelry shop, her eyes glued to the display case inside the window. She was looking for the ring priced at seven and a half *wŏn* she had set her heart on, but it was nowhere to be seen.

Dispirited, she plunged after some hesitation into the store, dragging Master Yun behind her.

"Irashaimase!"

All six salesmen sounded the Japanese greeting in unison as they gathered at the front of the store to take in the spectacle of this pair. Ch'unsim inquired from one of the salesmen about the whereabouts of the ring in question, using the few words of Japanese she had picked up at the *kisaeng* guild. The salesman listened patiently,

"I understand," he replied in fluent Korean. "But we've just sold the last one of those. But over here we have some similar ones. . . ."

He hurriedly opened the back of the showcase and took out a box studded with rings of all sizes. From among the red, blue, yellow, and black stones, he chose a red one and held it up for Ch'unsim to examine.

"This one is excellent. Much better than the one you were asking about. The setting is prettier and the stone's color is much nicer. I recommend this one."

Indeed, Ch'unsim agreed that this ring was prettier and better than the one she had seen earlier. When she tried it on her finger, it fit perfectly.

"Buy me this one, please."

She thrust the ring under Master Yun's nose. The price-tag was dangling at the end of a thread.

"Seven *wŏn* fifty *chŏn!* That's far too much!"

Master Yun lifted the train of his coat and was about to unfasten his purse, but then he stopped and turned to the salesman.

"Seven and a half is outrageous for this," he said. "You'll have to give a little discount."

"Sorry, sir! This one is ten *wŏn*, sir!"

"What? Ten? Why, just a minute now. How come you chose a ten-*wŏn* ring when you told me you'd get one for seven and a half?"

"Well, they're out of those, all sold out, so . . ."

"Then, no sale! Either we go elsewhere, or we can come back some other time!"

"No! I like this one. Buy it for me, please."

"No! It's out of the question!" Master Yun lifted his massive behind from the tiny stool where he had been sitting.

"Well, the difference is only two and a half *wŏn*, sir," the salesman said in an attempt to persuade Master Yun to relent.

"Please, sit back down," he continued. "This one is ten *wŏn*, but the quality of the stone is twice as good as the cheaper ring. Besides, the band is much thicker, sir."

"Still . . ."

"And, sir, if you are buying a ring for your grand-daughter, you might as well buy her a good one, sir."

The bastard deserved death. True, his intentions were innocent, but what could be worse than to call two lovers grandfather and little granddaughter? However, Master Yun was in no position to reprimand him; he was burning with shame. Ch'unsim, on the contrary, seemed to think it amusing and was wearing a bright, gay grin.

"This one, buy me this one. Or I won't!"

This last phrase Ch'unsim uttered with a meaningful air.

"Phew! What now? Phew! What now?"

Very reluctantly, Master Yun sat down again. His two deep sighs also had a meaningful air. The first signified surrender to Ch'unsim's extortion, and the second reflected his deeply felt shame at having been addressed as the girl's grandfather.

"So, now you're telling me that you must have this ring?"

"Yes."

"I'll tell you what. I'll buy this one, but the price is too high. How about a little discount?"

"No discount, sir. Ten *wŏn* for a ring of this quality is not at all expensive, sir."

"What do you mean not expensive? Stop quibbling! Here, I'll give you eight!"

"Sorry, sir, it won't do. At the full price, we have hardly any profit on the sale. But since you're a gentleman, I'll cut twenty *chŏn* off and let you have the ring for nine *wŏn* eighty *chŏn*."

"Moaning and groaning, moaning and groaning! I'll give you eight *wŏn*, eight and not a bit more!"

"You're not supposed to haggle over the price at a place like this!" Ch'unsim said in rebuke. "You're not dealing with a fishmonger!"

Under different circumstances, Master Yun would have drenched her in a rain of curses, but now that he had been taken for her grandfather he couldn't very well swear at her in public.

"You don't understand, little girl! No discount, no

bargain, that's the way of the world. I'm a man who haggles over everything, even over my tax assessments!"

The salesman grinned, thinking the old man a real wit.

With extreme reluctance, Master Yun removed some money from his purse, and after careful counting and recounting, checking and doublechecking, suddenly he said, in an alarmingly loud voice,

"Here! Eight *wŏn* fifty *chŏn!* That's the most I can pay!" Throwing words and money together at the salesman, Master Yun sprang from his seat.

"Let's go! It's done. Hurry up, now!" he said to Ch'unsim.

Aghast, the salesman jumped up and down and moved as if to seize Master Yun bodily. Another hour or so was spent arguing over the price. It was well past eleven when the couple left the store with the ring, purchased in the end for nine *wŏn* ten *chŏn.* It nearly took a fist fight to close the deal.

As the two left Ch'in Hill and crossed the square toward the streetcar stop, Ch'unsim kept looking down delightedly at the ring on her hand.

"Ch'unsim?"

"Yes?"

Ch'unsim turned to Master Yun with a smile, then glanced back at the ring.

"Are you happy, now that you've got your ring?"

"Well, not especially. . . ."

"You little bitch! Thanks to you I squandered my money and was humiliated, too!"

"Humiliated? How?"

"Why, didn't the bastard go on about me being your grandfather? And you being my granddaughter. . . ."

"Oh, that," Ch'unsim giggled.

"Anyhow, you'll do as I say now, won't you?"

"Yes."

"Uhm, you ought to, indeed. Well, later on tonight, eh?"

"Yes."

"Come early, you hear?"

"Yes."

"You mustn't disappoint me, understand?"

"Yes."

"Sure?"

"Don't worry."

"Uhm."

"By the way, Master?"

"What now?"

"Why don't we go to Mitsukoshi Department Store for some nannzi?"

"Nannzi? What the hell is nannzi, anyway?"

"It's a Western lunch, they call it 'nannzi.' "

"A Western lunch?"

"Yes, it's delicious."

"No way! Don't mention that rotten Western food."

"Why not?"

"I heard people praising Western food, so I went to one of those what-d'you-call-em places and tried it, and I tell you, it was a waste of money. I almost choked to death!"

"Ha, ha, ha . . . how come?"

"Why, they give you a thing like a rake to eat with!"

Had it not been for this unfortunate experience, Master Yun might have been dragged along by Ch'unsim and have had an opportunity to expound faithfully on the superiority of the Korean tradition in the course of a Western meal, but alas, due to his antagonism toward the so-called "meal with a rake," the opportunity never materialized.

As he bid goodbye to Ch'unsim at Chongno Intersection, Master Yun made sure he got several more assurances that she would come that evening without fail. And no sooner had he arrived back at his residence than Tadpole showed up with Mr. Kang, the man who was to borrow money from Master Yun against a draft. Since Taebok had already cleared him, Master Yun directly wrote out a check for the five-thousand-*wŏn* draft. Tadpole got a hundred and five *wŏn* as a commission, of course. Having sent Mr. Kang and Tadpole on their way, Master Yun was content at the thought that he had already made nine hundred and forty-five *wŏn* and the day was still young.

But . . . Yun Ch'angsik had blown four thousand five hundred *wŏn* at mahjong the night before, Chongsu had been defrauded by Pyongho to the tune of two thousand *wŏn,* and soon Chongsu would arrive to extract two thousand *wŏn* from his grandfather, so that about eight thousand *wŏn,* almost ten times the profit over which Master Yun was gloating, had vanished into thin air. In reality, then, Master Yun had suffered grievous losses that day. One might say a corner of the Great Wall had been gnawed away, but, of course, none of this had yet come to Master Yun's attention.

Once more, the pleasant thought of a rendezvous with Ch'unsim later that day made Master Yun's mouth water, and he was so intoxicated by this prospect that he forgot all about lunch, though the siren went off at noon as always.

At the sound of footsteps in the front yard, Master Yun casually looked out the window and there, to his unspeakable horror, he saw a pair of Western pants rushing in. So startled was he that he leapt up in an instant, ready to take refuge in the inner precincts of the house.

In recent years Master Yun had had hardly any visits from the so-called Western suits, but on the rare occasions when they did show up, he was invariably scared out of his wits.

Men, without exception, tend to be stricken with fear on suddenly encountering a snake. Instinctively they assume a wary attitude of self-defense. Some scholars have explained this phenomenon by saying that our ancient forebears over millions of years, from the earliest prehistoric *homo sapiens*, lived in terror, constantly battling against reptiles in an age in which reptiles were dominant, and so with the passage of time this vigilant instinctual fear became deeply embedded in human nature and today still runs in the blood of all mankind.

A plausible conjecture— and the terrified reaction exhibited by Master Yun to the Western suits, which was, first and foremost, to seek sanctuary, could be interpreted in a similar vein.

Subsequent to the Year of the Sheep, there had been a number of times when he had been attacked by those young men in Western suits: the black eye of a gun barrel aimed straight at his chest, robbed of money with his eyes wide open . . . and the memory of that torturous interrogation by the police during the course of reporting the robbery in detail . . . that he was widely known in the area as a man of wealth didn't necessarily evoke suspicion of conspiracy with the Western suits, and the police had merely been conducting a routine investigation necessary to track down and arrest the criminals. However, the process was agonizing for both sides due to the self-contradictory responses of Master

Yun, who already was half out of his mind from the sheer fright of the experiences.

Nothing in this world could make Master Yun shudder and grind his teeth like those men in Western suits.

Apart from these dangerous callers, there were also the insurance salesmen. This was a hardship often endured by the well-to-do, and Master Yun was no exception. Actually, he himself was disqualified from coverage due to his advanced age, but they still pestered him to purchase insurance policies for his son or his grandsons. Master Yun's answer to these importunate requests was quite poignant.

"Listen, young man!" he would say. "How can you ask me so blatantly to apply for insurance coverage for my son or my grandsons? You know very well that I can't buy policies and then sit here praying for them to die so that I can collect!"

But most insurance salesmen are not shooed away by such arguments, and most of them would go right on pestering him like leeches.

Yet another class of visitors abhorred by Master Yun were those soliciting donations of various sorts. Usually they came as promoters of some educational enterprise, or seekers of temporary relief for flood victims, or workers for some charity fund. After relating at length the full story, they would request a contribution. And Master Yun, having listened to the whole story, would answer nonchalantly,

"That's all good work, surely. No doubt everyone should do his share. . . . As for me, however, I've been relieving hundreds of poor people every year for the past several decades, so I don't see that I'll be committing any crime if I don't participate in your particular beneficial project!"

"Indeed! What a praiseworthy man you are! What kind of relief work have you been undertaking, sir?"

Struck by the departure from what they had heard about the old man, the callers would feel obliged to inquire into the nature of Master Yun's philanthropy.

"Well, I earn about ten thousand bags of rice annually, and there are close to a thousand tenant farmers on my estates. So I make my farmland available to provide a living for a thousand tenants, and if that's not relief, and on a grand scale at that, I don't know what is!"

At this, most sensible souls would chuckle under their breath and hasten to change the subject, but the slow-witted would be deeply impressed and would ask,

"Why, then, you mean you're parceling out your land to poor farmers without charging any rent? I'm truly impressed, sir!"

"What! How am I to live if I don't charge rent? Good gracious, tell me, is there a single idiot in the whole wide world who gives his land to others for their free use?"

Such was Master Yun's indignant rebuttal. The listener might take it as a jest of some kind, or as sheer nonsense, but Master Yun himself scarcely could have been more serious.

That a landowner's provision of his land to tenant farmers was a highly benevolent act, a virtuous deed of philanthropy, was a stock argument long cherished by Master Yun. Such an argument was not at all unreasonable in the terms of his logic of sensitivity. The assertion that the land was his property played a key role in the construction of his theory, and the governing fact under this methodology was that while the farmers— Kim, Ch'oe, Yi, Ch'ae, whoever— all competed with one another for the right to work as tenants on a certain piece of his farmland, the right inevitably fell only to one of the four. Since it was entirely up to the landlord to give it to Ch'oe, say, instead of Kim, Yi or Ch'ae, Ch'oe ought to feel only gratitude for the extraordinary dispensation awarded him by the landlord. Such more or less was Master Yun's rationale for claiming to be a philanthropist by virtue of his disposition of tenancy rights.

Accordingly, Master Yun was adamant in adhering to his philosophy of never donating a single *chŏn* to any charity run by civilians, or to natural disaster relief funds, though he made exceptions for institutions he particularly admired such as the police, to whom he had once made a contribution large enough to fund a martial arts hall. Thus the only kind of pestering he still encountered was the men in Western suits who occasionally turned up at his home.

After some twenty years of bitter experience in the country dealing with various threats, assaults, and raw deals from the Western suits, Master Yun had developed a second instinct of survival, one which made him automatically react with absolute revulsion and antagonism against any man in a Western suit. That was why he had sprung up to hide the moment he spotted a pair of trousers crossing the front yard, but he was a little too slow and the Western suit was quick, so before Master Yun could make a move the door had already been opened.

Master Yun was much relieved when a swift turn of his head revealed that it was not a stranger in a Western suit, but he was angry all the same for having been terrified for no reason.

"You! I should have your balls cut off! Why the hell

did you sneak in like that? You could cough at least!"

It was Chongsu, fresh from his night of debauchery. Curses from his grandfather he regarded as routine, so he attached no particular significance to this outburst. He just made an extra deep bow before kneeling down before his grandfather.

"What brings you to Seoul again?"

"I've some business to take care of . . ."

"I know your kind of business! You're here to rob me of my money, aren't you? Well, if you have money on your mind, you might as well get out of my sight right now!"

Checkmated, Chongsu was beaten before his first move. For a while he just sat there speechless, eyes cast down at the floor.

It was a situation, Master Yun knew, in which he should keep feigning anger, so the old man changed the subject to another he could use to berate Chongsu.

"What in the world is going on with you and that county magistracy?" he continued, banging his pipe on the ashtray. "How's it coming, anyway, eh? I'll have to wait until my grandson has a grandson before you get the post! To hell with it!"

Actually, Master Yun was quite relaxed about the matter, since it was a ten-year project, but it would be far better if Chongsu attained the magistracy in less than ten years, so he pressed his grandson at every opportunity, as one whips a galloping horse. This outburst, however, gave Chongsu an idea, a clever ruse to siphon some cash out of his grandfather.

"You needn't worry about that, Grandfather. As a matter of fact, that's what brought me to Seoul, and . . ."

"Really? That's the first good news I've heard from you in some time! So? Are you on the verge of a magistracy?"

Master Yun instantly mellowed and seemed in a very good mood. The old man was as innocent as a child.

"Looks like there'll soon be an official announcement of an opening for a major post!"

"Is that so? Really?"

"Yes, Grandfather."

"I can ask for no more! And when will you be promoted to a magistracy?"

"Once you hold a major post, the rest is easy!"

"Still, it'll probably take several years at least, won't it?"

"About four or five, I imagine. But then, you see . . ."

"What is it?"

"I need about two thousand *wŏn* to make the most of this chance. I don't want things to go awry."

Master Yun jumped up in fury. Inside he was picturing his grandson as a dignified noble, dressing him up in splendid attire, something like the uniforms high officials used to wear in the old days, with gold stripes on the sleeves and a gilded sword at his belt— true, that particular uniform was a thing of the past, but the gold stripes were still around, a single stripe for a junior officer and a double stripe for a county magistrate. Chongsu bringing up the abominable subject of money made his rage flare up again.

"I should have your balls cut off! You came here for no other reason than to sweet talk me out of my money! I can see right through you, through and through! Why, if the deal is almost set, why the hell do you need two thousand now? What the hell for?"

"I'm not asking for it to spend on myself!"

"If you won't spend it, who will? Some monk in Yŏsan?"

"I need it to buy a gift, a diamond ring!"

"What? Where on this earth is there a two-thousand-*wŏn* ring? And even if there is, a man wearing such a thing on his finger is bound to be struck dead by lightning! Is that why you want money, to give away such a ring as a present? I don't care how grand the man is, anybody who wears such a thing will rot as soon as he dies. Tell me, now, if that doesn't make you deserve to be struck by lightning! I've seen a few rings myself, and a perfectly nice one only costs nine *wŏn* ten *chŏn*. Whose idea was this, anyway? Did you think of it yourself, or did someone put you up to it?"

"The old county magistrate suggested it to me. You see, last time he was in Seoul, he ran into Mr. Ikeda. You know Mr. Ikeda, don't you? The official at the Home Affairs Desk of the Government-General, that Ikeda!"

"So?"

"The old magistrate ran into Mr. Ikeda as he was walking into Mitsukoshi Department Store with his wife and children. Mr. Ikeda seemed very pleased at meeting the old magistrate, and also he asked after me, saying he hadn't forgotten my case. . . . After that, they walked around together inside the store, doing some window-shopping. They happened to drop by a jeweler's, and when a two-thousand-*wŏn* ring was taken out to show them, Mrs. Ikeda couldn't seem to take her eyes off it. And Mr. Ikeda smiled and said he wished he could buy it for her, but he just didn't have the money. The wife was visibly crestfallen. The old magistrate told me that if only he'd bought that ring and given it to her on the spot as a gift, that would've had a far greater impact than a ten-thousand-*wŏn* gift in other circumstances. But he didn't have enough money on him, and, anyway, the sum was too great for him to manage . . ."

"In other words, you mean, the magistrate recommended that you buy the ring and send it to the Ikedas as a gift?"

"Yes. Especially since my case is now moving smoothly toward the final stage, he said it'd be very advantageous for me to do it. . . ."

Master Yun was silent for a while, puffing away on his pipe. In a way it sounded like a plausible story, but then again it could have been another instance of Chongsu's hocus-pocus. In the end, he came to the conclusion that he'd be better off giving the money despite the risk of being swindled, for he didn't want to put the whole project in jeopardy by mistaking a true story for a fake and so failing to offer that accursed gift.

"Damned if I know what to believe! All I have on me is a thousand *wŏn.* Take all of it and you can buy a gift or whatever; do what you think will work. I give up!"

As he himself often proclaimed, Master Yun was a man who even haggled over his taxes, so it was only natural for him to cut in half the bribery outlays requested by his grandson. Chongsu, however, well aware of this propensity of his grandfather, had purposely doubled his request and had managed to outwit Master Yun and lay hands on the thousand *wŏn* he wanted.

Master Yun summoned Taebok, wrote out a personal check for a thousand *wŏn,* and sent him to cash it for Chongsu. In his heart he felt empty and distressed, thinking that the nine hundred and forty-five *wŏn* he had earned that day was already slipping through his fingers, taking fifty-five more with it to boot.

Seek Not Far for the Agent of Your Doom

In the early days when he was better known as Toad Yun and his father was known as Horseface Yun Yonggyu, Master Yun had stood by the corpse of his father, who had been mercilessly murdered by bandits, his eyes trained on a sky reddened by the blazing granary.

"Will this stinking world never end?" he had shrieked.

"Let everyone else go to hell!"

Half a century had already passed since that curse of indignation at the heartlessness of the world, that grand declaration of war on life. And in the end, indeed, victory was what Master Yun had won. But now . . .

All the members of the family, except for Ko, whom Master Yun detested, had gathered in the main room to accord a proper greeting to Chongsu. Master Yun sat on the warm side of the floor, while Chongsu took a place facing the back wall. They were about to be served lunch.

"Kyŏngson's father, you better pull yourself together!" This was an admonition to Chongsu, but Master Yun, conscious of the observers, tempered his tone by using the seemliest form of address, "Kyŏngson's father."

"I say you should pull yourself together for I'm inclined to think that in many respects you're inferior to your younger brother, Chonghak! That boy's got real talent. He's very industrious, not at all a loose sort like you, and besides, in a few years he'll be graduating from the University. He graduates year after next, doesn't he?"

"Yes sir."

"Right. Hmmm, so he'll be out of school in a couple of years, and with three or four more years of hard work, that boy's going to be what he set out as his goal. People nowadays like to use that word 'goal,' don't they?

"A goal . . . a purpose in life, to become a police officer, then, before you know it, he's a police chief! Understand?"

"Yes sir."

"So, you should pull yourself together and hurry up and become a county magistrate, you hear? Why, your younger brother will be a proud police chief while you, the older brother, are still a lowly clerk! How can you bear such shame, eh? Why, if the two of you become a police chief and a county magistrate, you'll be the ones in luxury and glory, not me! It's for your own sake that I keep grinding at you like this; there's not a fish's tit in it for me! You understand?"

"Yes sir."

"Chonghak, that boy is something else! Even as a child he was a gem, gifted and well mannered, and as he grew up he always heeded my advice . . . I have faith in that boy, I certainly do. Since last year he's been spending a bit too much money, but it's a pittance compared to what you spend. Besides, being a spendthrift is no defect in a man as long as he has firmness of character, not the sort of looseness and carelessness I see in you. That's why when he wrote me last month asking for five hundred *wŏn* for some urgent matter, I sent it right off without asking a question!"

At that moment, a gentle cough was heard out in the front yard. Yun Ch'angsik, who had awakened only a little while before, was reluctantly putting in an appearance to inform his father of the telegram he had received from Tokyo the night before.

Ch'angsik casually acknowledged his son, Chongsu, who was coming outside onto the stepping stones to greet him. And he sent a silent greeting to his two daughters-in-law who were also coming out to welcome him. The Seoul Mistress, who came only as far as the hall, exchanged a murmur of recognition with her brother as he made his way into the main room. Once inside, he bowed deeply to his father, received a deep bow from his son, and a salute from his stepbrother, T'aesik. When these ceremonies were over, he knelt down in the corner of the room.

"The sun's going to rise in the west!"

This was Master Yun's snide way of noting the most uncommon fact that his son not only had paid a visit without a summons, but had actually entered all the way inside the house.

"What brings you here? Need money?"

"There was a telegram from Tokyo . . ."

Had the family hierarchy been inverted, with Yun Ch'angsik in the role of gentle father and Master Yun in that of rash and impudent son, it would have been a perfect scene.

"From Tokyo? A telegram?"

"Chonghak's been arrested by the Metropolitan Police!"

"Whhhaaat?!!"

Great was the volume of Master Yun's wail, but still greater was the impact he made as he leaped up and heaved back down, nearly breaking through the *ondol* floor of the room. Of course, everyone in the assembled household was astonished in their own way, each to a different degree.

As if he had received a blow on the back of his head from a heavy club, Master Yun was stupefied, wide-eyed, speechless. He sat there motionless for a long while. At last he recovered his senses; his posture grew tense.

"Now, what are you saying?" he growled. "What are you talking about? Eh? Speak up!"

"The telegram seems to be from one of his friends, and since it's a telegram I can't tell very much from it."

Yun Ch'angsik removed the telegram from his vest pocket and handed it to his father. Master Yun half-snatched it away and, after a long look at it, began to read it out loud. The original was in Japanese, of course, a language unknown to Master Yun, but he was reading the translation by Min, the servant at Ch'angsik's house.

"Chonghak taken into custody by Metropolitan Police in connection with ideology! So it says, well, tell me, what does this mean?"

"I suppose it means that Chonghak has been arrested for an ideological offense!"

"Ideological offense? What's that?"

"The boy was involved in socialism . . ."

"Whhhaaat?!"

Screaming still louder than before, Master Yun almost flung himself flat on his back. With difficulty he managed to regain his balance. Earlier he had been stupefied; now he was nearly fainting. He felt as dizzy as if the ground where he sat was falling into a bottomless pit.

The extreme reaction exhibited by Master Yun was not, however, in any way due to his concern for his beloved grandson Chonghak, or for his condition. The simple fact that Chonghak had become a socialist enraged the old man far more than if he had been raided by a thousand Western suits of the sort that marauded in the old days. Moreover, Master Yun was petrified.

The Emperor of Qin, on hearing a prophecy that the agent responsible for the future fall of the Qin Empire would be Ho, ordered the construction of the Great Wall to shield his northern frontiers from the barbarians of Ho. And blessed was the Emperor of Qin, for he died without learning that the agent who brought about the fall of the Empire was not the Ho barbarians, but his own son, whose name was also Ho.

"What do you mean, socialism?"

Ready to eat someone alive, Master Yun thundered on, "So! The bastard is into socialism!"

"As a matter of fact, I sensed something of the kind when he was in Seoul last summer."

"Then it's true! My God, it's true!"

Beads of sweat rolled down Master Yun's forehead onto his cheeks.

"The bastard deserves to be hanged! Skinning him alive isn't enough! I send him to become a police chief, and now he's in jail, eh? The little son of a bitch should be drawn and quartered! What's socialism to him that he should take it up? Why the hell does the son of a rich man want to join the gangsters?"

Nobody dared to take an audible breath. Standing or sitting, all hung their heads low, and when Master Yun paused for a moment, a dead silence reigned in the room.

"In this wonderful, splendid world! Such a wonderful world . . ."

Banging the floor with his fist, Master Yun went on bellowing in a voice like the mating call of an ox,

"The bandits are all gone now, aren't they? And the chieftains too! The age of doom, when thieves took your property, and your life was worth no more than a fly's, those days are behind us! Look around you! There's a policeman on every street corner, and every village is governed fair and square! What more can you want than this?

"Don't ever forget to thank your lucky stars we live in this wonderful world, where the Japanese have mobilized a huge army, hundreds of thousands of soldiers, to protect us Koreans! It's a world of peace where we can keep what is ours and live in comfort! Peace under heaven, that's what it is! Peace under heaven, you understand? And now, a rich man's son, born into a world of peace under heaven, why should he join up with a bunch of gangsters who'll bring ruin to the world? Why not just enjoy the life of a rich man in a foreign land? Why not, eh?"

Master Yun pounded the floor with his fist and scrambled abruptly to his feet. So frantically violent was his behavior that it seemed he might undergo a seizure at any minute. In truth, the members of the Yun family were not only startled by the sudden banging on the floor, they couldn't help thinking that the old man was on the verge of losing his mind entirely.

"The bastard should be chopped to pieces! I'll write to the police, tell them to put him in prison for a hundred years! Wait and see! I'd planned to leave him three thousand bags. Well, now, I'll sell off that land and donate the proceeds to the police, the police who hunt down those bastards and throw them in prison! Damn him!"

These last words were more like weeping than speech.

"Peace under heaven! Peace under heaven!"

Master Yun stamped out to the main hall in a rage, followed by Ch'angsik, who had risen from his knees, and by Chongsu.

"The bastard son of a rich family joining the socialist gangsters! Damn him!"

Master Yun's wild shrieks of "Damn him!" gradually grew fainter as he moved toward his room. Yet that terrible roar somehow kept echoing ominously in the ears of the family members left behind speechless, gazing at each other's clouded faces, restlessly searching for somewhere else to go. They were like soldiers compelled to face up to the death of their commander . . .

Glossary

Amitabha	The deity—Buddha of Infinite Light —of Pure Land Buddhism, a simple form of worship in which the repetition of the chant "*Nammu Amit'a Pul*" was held to facilitate rebirth as an immortal in the Western Paradise or "Pure Land" where the Amitabha Buddha reigns. The great Silla dynasty monk Wŏnhyo (617–686) played a major role in propagating devotion to Amitabha among the Korean masses.
changgi	A war simulation board game of Chinese origin similar in type to Western chess.
chŏngjong wine	A rice wine similar to *sake*, more refined than *makkŏlli*.
Ch'usa, Soch'i and Misan	are the posthumous names by which three famous Chosŏn dynasty painters are known.

"darting birds" A game of chance and form of gambling, in which winning turned on choosing among several small birds at which the players cast darts.

"familiar level of speech" The Korean language is highly stratified with words and grammatical structures differing depending upon social relations among speaker, addressee and referent. Five levels are commonly distinguished: (1) intimate, (2) familiar or informal, (3) polite, (4) formal, and (5) honorific.

Hwalbindang A name generally applied to groups of impoverished bandits or thieves whose avowed aim was to rob the rich and distribute their wealth to the poor. The term is encountered to describe the cohorts of the mythic Hong Kil-Dong, a Robin Hood-like leader whose *Hwalbindang* band was the scourge of corrupt and greedy landlords and magistrates. Although the *Hwalbindang* at times in Korean history may have coalesced on the scale of regional peasant uprisings or jacqueries, in normal usage *Hwalbindang* refers to small spontaneous groups rather than to a large, organized movement.

kayagŭm

A traditional Korean stringed instrument, similar to a Chinese zither, consisting of a wooden sounding board about 1.5 meters long, played upon the seated musician's lap. Most *kayagŭm* had about 10 or 12 strings, each with its own movable bridge which suspends the string more than three centimeters off the board. The strings are struck or plucked with one hand while the other bends notes by fretting.

kisaeng

Traditional female entertainers, in many respects comparable to Japanese *geisha,* who from an early age were trained in music, dancing, painting, and other fine arts. Some served as courtesans or as concubines to *yangban*; however, *kisaeng* were not common prostitutes. Traditionally, *kisaeng* as well as their children suffered from various forms of social stigmatization and exclusion, though many were highly literate and some *kisaeng* made important contributions to Korean art and literature.

Koryŏ— "fall of Koryŏ . . . the iron . . . eaten by oxen."

In folk culture, the demise of a dynasty was generally regarded as being prefigured in uncanny portents of apocalypse. According to popular Korean legend, as the Koryŏ dynasty (A.D. 932–1392) neared its end, there was wide circulation of rumored sightings of *P'ulgasari*, an imaginary iron-eating beast with the body of a bear, the trunk of an elephant, the eyes and tail of a bull ox, and the legs of a tiger.

makkŏlli

A traditional Korean wine made from fermented grain, usually rice, sweet rice or barley. *Makkŏlli* is milky-white and thick in consistency, with a relatively low alcohol content. It is cheaper than refined rice wines and readily made at home, and thus has been a favorite of peasants and other poor folk.

Manchurian Incident

In 1930, due in part to the deepening global economic crisis, a faction in the Japan military staged an incident by which an explosion on the Manchurian Railway was attributed to China. The incident was used to justify a military incursion. This led the following year to the establishment by the Japanese of the puppet state of Manchukuo. China protested to the League of Nations, and a compromise was suggested by the Lytton Investigative Mission, but Japan declined the intermediation and in 1933 withdrew from the League of Nations.

nyang An old Chosŏn dynasty monetary unit, equal to one hundred of the old copper *sangp'yŏngt'ongbo* (q.v.). Also a unit of weight for silver and other metals.

ondol A heating system commonly used in traditional Korean houses, whereby heat was circulated from charcoal burners through passages constructed beneath under the lacquered paper floors of the sitting and sleeping rooms of the house.

paduk A board game of territorial possession and capture, better known in the West as *go.* This game has long been and still remains very popular among Korean men of the educated classes.

p'yŏng A traditional Korean measure of area used for land and buildings. One *p'yŏng* equals about 3.3 square meters. A hectare (about 2.5 acres) of land is on the order of 3,000 *p'yŏng.*

sangp'yŏngt'ongbo The name, which in literal translation is "Ever-Normal Circulating

Treasure," of copper coins which, from their first minting is 1633, were the basic cash currency of Chosŏn dynasty Korea. These coins were struck with a hole in their center to facilitate stringing them together. The bimetallic copper/ silver monetary system of the Chosŏn period, with the value of coinage fixed first in terms of in- trinsic value of the minted metal and later in terms of a flat rate of conversion into rice, went through many failed reforms. After 1910 the Japanese imposed the *yen* as the basic unit of account, thus the old *sangp'yŏngt'ongbo* were only as valuable as their intrinsic cooper content.

sijo	A genre of Korean verse dating to the Koryŏ period, with a conven- tional three line structure: the first two lines each are composed of 14 or 15 syllables in the form 3-4-3(4)- 4, and the closing line composed of fifteen syllables in the form 3-5-4-3.
Tongdaemun	The name, meaning Great East Gate (as Namdaemun means Great South Gate and Sŏdaemun means Great West Gate), of one of the mas- sive stone gateways to the ancient walled city of Seoul. Metonymically,

the name also is used for the Seoul precincts to the east of the city center.

So Daesŏng   The hero of a Chosŏn dynasty prose narrative, *The Tale of So Daesŏng,* who is famous for his remarkable capacity for extended sleep.

T'ongyŏng kat   A small black top hat with a wide, round brim traditionally worn by male *yangban* (q.v.). *Kat* generally were woven from horsehair, and were tied securely to the head with a drawstring under the chin. T'ongyŏng is a city in South Kyŏngsang-do renowned for the fine quality of the *kat* produced by its craftsmen.

wŏn/chŏn   In the modern Korean monetary system, the basic unit of account is the *wŏn,* which circulated in the 1930s in the form of paper notes in units of 1, 10, 100, etc. One *wŏn* equaled one hundred *chŏn.* The Japanese *yen* corresponded to *wŏn* and Japanese *sen* to *chŏn* (differing pronunciations of the same Chinese character). *Chŏn* coins, as noted elsewhere in the text, replaced the old *sangp'yŏngt'ongbo* (q.v.), at a conversion rate of five of the old coins per *chŏn.*

yangban

In traditional Korea, the landed aristocratic class which by inheritance enjoyed an exclusive right to a Classical Confucian education, to prebendal income as tax farmers for the monarch, and to local magistracies and posts as advisers to the court. The term *yangban* is contrasted to *sangnom* or "common folk."